Southern Africa

New and Future Titles in the
Indigenous Peoples of Africa Series Include:

Southern Africa

Cynthia L. Jenson-Elliott

LUCENT
BOOKS®

THOMSON
———✴———™
GALE

San Diego • Detroit • New York • San Francisco • Cleveland • New Haven, Conn. • Waterville, Maine • London • Munich

Cover image: Women and children of the San Bushmen ethnic
group trek through the Kalihari desert to gather food.

LIBRARY OF CONGRESS CATALOGING-IN-PUBLICATION DATA

Jenson-Elliott, Cynthia L.
    Southern Africa / by Cynthia L. Jenson-Elliott.
        p. cm. — (Indigenous peoples of Africa)
Summary: Covers lifestyles of Southern African ethnic groups, Arab and European
influences, religion, culture, and current problems facing Southern Africa.
Includes bibliographical references (p.) and index.
    ISBN 1-59018-084-4 (alk. paper)
   1. Ethnology—Africa, Southern—Juvenile literature.   2. Human geography—
Africa, Southern—Juvenile literature.   3. Africa, Southern—Juvenile literature.
[1. Ethnology—Africa, Southern. 2. Human geography—Africa, Southern.
3. Indigenous peoples—Africa, Southern. 4. Africa, Southern.] I. Title. II. Series.
    DT1054 .J46 2003
    305.8′00968—dc21

            2002008907

Printed in the United States of America

Contents

Foreword

Long recognized as the birthplace of humankind, the continent of Africa has, for centuries, been inhabited by a diverse population. Physically separated by deserts, valleys, and lush forests, the people of Africa succeeded in creating unique cultural identities and lifestyles that perfectly suited the lands on which they lived. The Maasai of East Africa's Great Rift Valley, for instance, became skilled pastoralists, using young warriors to build and protect large herds of cattle and goats on the arid plains of the east. And the Ibo of Nigeria adapted their clothing and shelter-building techniques to suit life in a tropical climate.

These isolated cultures collided with outside influences sometime before A.D. 100 as Arab traders landed on African shores, and again during the fifteenth century with the arrival of Europeans. The traders came to Africa in search of valuables: gold, ivory, and diamonds. They found these items and more. One of the continent's most profitable resources turned out to be the Africans themselves. Thus began the international slave trade, which dispersed Africans to countries around the world.

During the five centuries that followed, Africa's population was indelibly influenced by the traders and their descendants. Islam and Christianity, religions of the Arabs and Europeans, merged with traditional African beliefs. Furthermore, the power and influence of the traders—the Europeans in particular—supplanted local tribal law and led to hundreds of years of imperial rule. Yet, in spite of these influences and changes, the people of Africa managed to sustain their individual cultures and ways of life. Languages, rites of passage, tribal legends—all remained unique to the tribes that practiced them.

The *Indigenous Peoples of Africa* series examines that diversity by presenting a complex and realistic picture of the various tribal cultures. Each book in the series offers historical perspectives as well as a view of contemporary life in all of the continent's regions. The series examines family life, spirituality, art, interaction with outsiders, work, education, and the challenges faced by Africa's population today.

In many cases, those challenges are daunting. AIDS and other infectious diseases wipe out entire villages. Many African children never attend school. Human rights violations abound. Refugees of tribal warfare starve in substandard camps. Government censorship prevents citizens and journalists from speaking out against corrupt political leaders. However, even on this continent devastated by famine, ravaged by disease, and torn by war, the African people endure, bound by tradition and guided by history.

Africans also catch glimpses of a bright future. In western Africa, twenty-first century political leaders are endorsing democratic forms of government. In Kenya, a mobile library brings books to people living in isolated rural regions. And in Ethiopia, the current government sponsors training programs aimed at teaching the local population farming and agricultural techniques.

The *Indigenous Peoples of Africa* series attempts to capture both the Africans' history and their future, their rich culture, and their current challenges. Fully documented primary and secondary source quotations enliven the text. Sidebars highlight events, personalities, and traditions. Bibliographies provide readers with ideas for further research. Each book in this dynamic series provides students with a wealth of information as well as launching points for further research.

Southern Africa, Land of Extremes

Southern Africa, the region of the continent south of the Zambezi River is unique in its extremes, both in geography and culture. Consisting of the nations of Angola, Botswana, Lesotho, Mozambique, Namibia, the Republic of South Africa, Swaziland, and Zimbabwe, southern Africa supports a wide variety of ecosystems, or plant and animal communities, and human lifestyles.

The ecosystems of southern Africa include both the world's harshest and most livable environments. In the southwestern reaches of southern Africa lie the deserts: the rolling dunes of the Namib Desert and the dry brushlands of the south-central Kalihari Desert. These baking deserts, while seemingly inhospitable, provide a home to a rich community of plants and animals often found nowhere else in the world. Rich plant and animal communities also characterize the northeast corner of southern Africa. This area, crisscrossed by large rivers such as the Zambezi and Limpopo and their tributaries, is home to

humid tropical woodlands and the rare and endangered plants and animals that inhabit them.

Between the tropical woodlands and deserts lie a variety of ecosystems. Much of southern Africa is covered with dry grasslands and scrublands scattered with thorn bushes and small shrubs. The grassland and scrubland, characterized by moderate rainfall, are called the "veld" or grazing area. Higher elevations are called the highveld, while lower elevations are known as the lowveld. The veld has long supported the populations of large mammals that Africa is famous for—elephants, various kinds of hoofed animals, and predators such as lions and cheetahs. Today it also is home to domestic animals such as cattle and sheep that graze the plains and hills.

The low rolling hills of the northern highveld reach mountainous elevations in the south, becoming the rocky and rugged Drakensburg Mountains of the southeast. The Drakensburgs separate the highveld of the interior from the lower elevations of the coast. The southern African coast itself is among the most varied on the continent. The coastal strip ranges from the parched dunes of the western Namib Desert to the warm and dry Mediterranean forest and scrublands at the southern tip of the continent, to the richer, rainier agricultural lands on the river deltas of the east coast.

The Resources of the Region

The rich ecosystems of the coast and interior of southern Africa extend off the coast, as well. A teeming fishery fills the waters surrounding the southern reaches of Africa, providing a natural resource which has supported both the ancient cultures of the region and today's modern nations, such as Namibia and Mozambique.

Southern Africa's rich fishery is not the only source of natural wealth for the region, however. Mineral resources—gold, diamonds, tin, and other metals and precious jewels—provide essential revenue for nations whose burgeoning populations present great financial challenges. Mining provides not only revenue through sales but also employment for the people of southern Africa, thousands of whom cross national boundaries to work in the mines of neighboring countries every year.

The people of southern Africa are perhaps the region's most important natural resource, and they are as diverse culturally and economically as the landscape. Southern Africans of all ethnicities use their cultural strengths to adjust to the changing economic and political landscape of the

The vast deserts of southern Africa are home to some plants and animals that are found nowhere else on earth.

Johannesburg, South Africa, in extreme contrast to the desert, is a city of prosperous businesses and lush suburbs.

region. The San Bushmen of the Kalihari Desert of Botswana, for example, continue to participate in one of the world's earliest lifestyles, hunting wild animals and gathering wild food plants while struggling to make a living within radically altered political boundaries. At the opposite extreme are wealthy white businessmen in the suburbs of Johannesburg, South Africa, who are learning to expand their businesses in a world no longer so sharply divided between whites and blacks.

Between these two extremes is an enormous and growing multiracial and multiethnic middle class, living in suburban and rural areas, farming and herding on the land, digging in mines, or working in ur-

ban factories, services, and industries. The growth of this middle class is both caused by and contributes to the mixing and changing of cultures in southern Africa. The ability to adjust to changing political and economic circumstances is one of the great strengths of the southern African people. As governments and markets changed over the centuries, southern African cultures maintained a dynamic balance, mixing and melding and finding ways to survive and flourish amid often chaotic events.

Cultural Diversity

The dynamic nature of culture and lifestyle in southern Africa is not new: The human history of southern Africa is rich with extremes, rife with conflict, and churning with change. Throughout history, as ethnic groups occupying neighboring lands mixed and intermarried, they shared cultural practices, words, and traditions, as well as political and economic systems. For this reason it often has been difficult for scientists to identify where one southern African "tribe" ends and another begins. Many scientists believe that, because of the active dynamics of African culture, the term "tribe" can be confusing and even misleading. According to Jocelyn Murray, editor of the *Cultural Atlas of Africa,* the word "tribe," as used by Western nations, is ill-defined and prejudicial because there is little agreement about what constitutes a tribe.

In pre-colonial times the peoples of Africa were divided into hundreds of different nationalities and ethnic groups, of greatly varying size and with great differences in culture and values. In some cases multi-ethnic states . . . encompassed many peoples under a single central political authority. In other cases, ethnicity was coterminus [ended in the same place as] the political unit, as in the 19th century kingdom of the Zulu of southern Africa, while at the other extreme there were ethnic groups . . . divided into many tiny independent political units, some no larger than a village. The European conquest lumped different peoples together in new ways in the colonial territories

of the early 20th century, and the modern independent states of Africa, as inheritors of the colonial boundaries, today seek to blend their various peoples together into single nations.[1]

But ethnic diversity has not disappeared with the creation of modern nations: Ethnic distinctions are alive and well. Because current cultures and lifestyles are often different from what they were in the past, sociologists (scientists who study societies) must use other tools to clarify ethnic identities. Many of these researchers believe that the most accurate way to identify African societies and ethnic groups is by the languages that they speak, for language can show where a group of people came from and to whom they are related. Sociologists have identified four main language families, or groups of languages sharing word roots and origins, in all of Africa. Two of these language families, Bantu and Khoisan, are found in southern Africa.

Khoisan speakers, who live throughout the Cape region and southwest Africa, are thought to be descendants of the earliest inhabitants of southern Africa. Today their languages, and the ethnic groups that speak them, number about twenty-six, with many additional subgroups speaking the same languages. Khoisan languages are distinctive for their use of a number of "clicking" sounds. The earliest Khoisan speakers were seminomadic pastoralists, or animal herders, and hunter-gatherers who hunted animals and gathered wild plant foods.

Southern Africa

Once they lived throughout southern Africa. Today they live mainly in southwest Africa and the Cape region. In the north and east they have been largely replaced by Bantu speakers who crossed into the region around the second century A.D.

Around A.D. 200, agriculturalists, or farmers, from western Africa crossed the Limpopo River and set down roots in southern Africa. These farmers spoke languages in the Bantu language family and used the resources of the land in a radically different way than the pastoralists and hunter-gatherers: They brought metalworking skills and used iron tools to till the soil and harvest crops.

Unlike their nomadic neighbors, the agriculturalists stayed put, developing agricultural communities, trade networks, and social systems which ultimately expanded to become the first complex political systems and kingdoms of the region. In the centuries preceding, and even coincidental with, the European occupation of southern Africa, dozens of Bantu-speaking African kingdoms vied for dominance in a region rich in natural resources.

Today nearly sixty Bantu languages are spoken by ethnic groups that continue to practice agriculture, herding, and mixed lifestyles in southern Africa. Bantu languages in southern Africa are divided into many subgroups, each representing many different ethnic groups. Speakers of the Nguni language group are among the most numerous. They include the Zulu and Xhosa of South Africa, the Swazi of Swaziland, and the Ndebele of Zimbabwe, all of whom once fought for territory in South Africa. Speakers of the Sotho language group include the Northern Sotho of northern South Africa, the Southern Sotho of Lesotho, and the Tswana and related ethnic groups in Botswana and Namibia.

Language Families of Southern Africa

Language Group	Ethnic Group	Country
Bantu		
Nguni	Zulu	South Africa
	Xhosa	South Africa
	Swazi	Swaziland
	Ndebele	Zimbabwe
Sotho	Northern Sotho	Northern South Africa
	Southern Sotho	Lesotho
	Tswana	Botswana and Namibia
Shona	Various	Zimbabwe and Mozambique
Tsonga	Various	Mozambique
Honanib	Herero	Northern Namibia and Southern Angola
Ovambo	Ovambo	
Umbundu	Umbundu	
Khoisan		
Various	Various	South Africa Cape, Namibia, Angola, and Botswana

Source: Atlas of the World's Languages.

Speakers of the Shona language group live in Zimbabwe and parts of Mozambique, while much of Mozambique is inhabited by speakers of Tsonga languages. In northern Namibia and southern Angola, speakers of three related Bantu language groups—the Herero, Ovambo, and Umbundu—share space with speakers of Khoisan languages.

Ties to the Past, Hope for the Future

While Khoisan-speaking and Bantu-speaking ethnic groups have mixed and intermingled, in many ways the cultures of individual ethnic groups remain distinct. Individuals in southern Africa today identify and value themselves as both citizens of a nation and members of an ethnic group. As editor Jocelyn Murray asserts in her *Cultural Atlas of Africa,* despite the blending of cultures and lifestyles that has marked African history, and despite the efforts of governmental leaders to create modern nations out of disparate peoples, "it is safe to say that the older ethnic ties remain potent forces in African life down to the present."[2]

These ethnic ties, which often extend across national boundaries, help the nations inhabiting southern Africa today maintain generally peaceful relations with their neighbors. United by a common history and a hope for the future, the governments of the region work together to create harmonious political and trading relationships. And in each nation, the cultural values and traditions passed on in each ethnic group gives each nation a breadth of talents and a dynamic creative energy that is vital to success in the global economy.

Chapter 1

Lifestyles of Southern African People

The people of southern Africa live diverse lifestyles uniquely suited to the varied climates and ecosystems of the region. Speaking numerous languages and possessing a multitude of cultural traits, the ethnic groups that have called southern Africa home since around A.D. 200 have one very important trait in common: They have all, at various points in their history, developed characteristic lifestyles to help them adapt to the natural environments of the region. And each of them, in the face of the changes wrought by modern political and economic realities, has adapted these traditional lifestyles to help them survive in today's world.

In the past, the traditional lifestyles of southern African ethnic groups were divided into three main groups—farmers, herders, and hunter-gatherers—with many ethnic groups using a mixture of these lifestyles to make a living. Lifestyle largely depended on the environment and climate in which a group lived. Areas with a great deal of rain were suitable to agriculture. Areas with less rainfall and good grazing land were used by pastoral ethnic groups. And the harshest, driest regions were inhabited by hunter-gatherers. In some areas, however, the environment made a mixed economy—a mixture of ways of making a living—desirable.

Mixed economies took many forms. Ethnic groups who lived along rivers farmed the fertile land in addition to fishing and using the rivers as trade routes. Ethnic groups who herded animals often became rich in livestock and used their surplus animals to develop a lively trade. And some agricultural ethnic groups developed such skills as weaving, ironwork, and even gold mining as a way to increase their wealth through trade.

Today most southern African ethnic groups continue to practice a mixed economy. In rural areas, tribes farm small plots of land, herd domestic animals, fish, and hunt. Some of these people travel long distances to work in mines, large-scale agriculture, and other industries to supplement

The "Coloured" Population of South Africa

Throughout southern Africa, due to the colonial past of the region, a large number of mixed-race individuals make their home in urban areas and in the countryside. In South Africa, those of mixed race are legally and administratively classified as "Coloured." While in the United States, the word "colored" is considered to be a derogatory, or insulting, pre–civil rights era reference to African Americans, in South Africa, the word "Coloured" is simply a common descriptive and legal term.

But who are the Coloured people of South Africa? In his 1973 book entitled *Coloured: A Profile of Two Million South Africans* author Al J. Venter asked a South African Coloured man what it meant to be classified as Coloured. The man replied,

"Problems, real problems. Who really knows what a Coloured is? They classify us, they categorize us according to their ideals and they keep us apart from the rest— in our own interests—we are told. Then they move us out of our homes, our villages and towns and our churches. But unlike Africans we are not Xhosa or Zulu or Sotho. We are South African. Our culture, our languages, even our way of life is South African. What else are we but South African?"

Today, people who identify themselves as Coloured make up nearly 9 percent of the South African population, or 3.6 million people, according to the yearly study *South Africa Survey 1999/2000*. During the apartheid era, the Coloured population was classified according to appearance, so children within the same family could have different designations, depending on the shade of their skin. During this period, under apartheid laws of segregation, Coloured people were restricted from marrying other races or living outside the areas designated as "Coloured" areas. Their professional development was also restricted by race, as only certain jobs and positions were classified as suitable for the "Coloured" population. As with all South Africans during that period, Coloured people were restricted in every aspect of their lives by the color of their skin.

During the apartheid era, Coloured South Africans faced restrictions based on their skin color, such as segregation on city buses.

their incomes. Sometimes, though, work in rural areas is difficult to find. Often, the unemployed migrate to urban areas looking for jobs.

Despite these modern mixed economies, remnants of traditional lifestyles are visible and help ethnic groups stay connected with their roots. Ethnic groups that traditionally herded cattle—the Herero of Namibia, for example—continue to have a strong relationship with cattle while also working in agriculture and mining. And groups that predominantly practiced agriculture—such as the Zulu of South Africa—continue to farm, either living in traditional agricultural villages in rural areas or maintaining small farm plots a distance from their urban homes. Even village-dwelling San Bushmen of Namibia continue to use their knowledge of plants and animals to hunt and gather wild plant food seasonally to add to their current livelihoods in farming, herding, or mining. These mixed lifestyles are typical of the lively dynamics of southern African ethnic identity.

Rural Lifestyles

Throughout much of southern Africa, most families rely on agriculture, or farming, to survive. In the agricultural villages of KwaZulu-Natal in South Africa, for example, and the nations of Swaziland and Zimbabwe, agriculture provides at least a partial living for millions of people. In fact, according to *South Africa Survey 1999/2000* (a yearly study), 70 percent of households in South Africa, including some in urban areas, have access to agricultural land and rely on farming to some degree to feed their families.

Life in agricultural villages follows a pattern dictated in part by tribal traditions. Among the Zulu in South Africa, for example, many people continue to live in traditional homesteads surrounded by agricultural land. Zulu homesteads generally consist of a fenced compound which contains the households of members of an extended family, plus granaries for storing grain and a fenced area, or kraal, for penning cattle and goats. Family compounds are often built near the compounds of other family members, so that one village area may contain many homesteads of an extended family.

In KwaZulu-Natal as well as other agricultural areas, small villages housing the goods and services necessary to rural life are often located within a short distance of homesteads. Today, villages often contain open-air marketplaces and transportation services as well as churches, medical clinics, schools, post offices, and police stations. Tiny shops sell life's necessities—knives and other tools, cloth, tea, and sugar—to residents who are able to afford them.

Rural villages are similar throughout southern Africa, even in areas that are home to predominantly pastoral tribes. Pastoralism, raising animals, is a common part of many southern Africans' livelihoods. Because the veld covers much of the region, herders have access to grazing land for domestic animals. Yet while more

Swazi farmers use oxen to plow their land. Many southern Africans continue this traditional practice and agricultural lifestyle.

than half of rural households own non-dairy cattle, and over 80 percent own some number of sheep or goats, no ethnic group in southern Africa today makes its living exclusively by herding. In fact, few ethnic groups in southern Africa have historically followed an exclusively pastoral lifestyle making their living solely from their domestic animals. The Herero, Bantu-speaking pastoralists of Namibia and Botswana, were traditionally the most exclusively pastoral of the ethnic groups in the region, with many of their cultural traditions reflecting their cattle-raising lifestyle. Today, however, the Herero herd cattle in addition to working in mines and farming. And their once seminomadic

herding lifestyle has largely been exchanged for a sedentary village life.

In Lesotho, home of the Southern Sotho people, the economy is mixed, but herding represents an important part of a family's income and is done largely by young boys, aged six to fifteen. According to a 2002 article in the *Los Angeles Times* newspaper,

Boys as young as 6 are sent to the mountains to look after livestock, including sheep, goats, cattle and donkeys. While some boys shepherd during the day and return home in the evening, many live away from home for months at a time in makeshift shelters that form so-called cattle posts.

"It's important to have a herd boy to take care of these precious [animals]," said Pius Fako Masupha, chief of Ha Mamathe, a settlement . . . where he estimates there are as many as 2,000 herd boys. "You will find a herd boy in each and every family that has cattle."[3]

In addition to cattle herding, Southern Sotho families also farm small inadequate plots of land, making their lifestyle, like that of so many other ethnic groups, a mixed economy.

Some creative residents of southern Africa use every lifestyle imaginable to make a living from the harsh land in which they live. The Kavango peoples, living near the Okavango River that borders Angola, Namibia, and Botswana, are an example of an ethnic group which uses mixed methods to earn a living. They rely on the rich fishery and other wildlife of the Okavango River. They also depend on the river for irrigation. The Kavango peoples have successfully practiced this mixed economy for hundreds of years.

One of the Kavango groups, the Gciriku people who live along the Okavango River in Angola, follow an annual cycle of subsistence in which men, women, and children all play a part in the work of sustaining the group. For men and women, part of the year is given to the planting and harvesting of crops while the remaining months are occupied with fishing. As additional sustenance, Gciriku children herd cattle and goats, and men hunt wild animals. Additionally, men often leave home to work as contract laborers in cities. With this mixed economy, the Gciriku are able to make an adequate living.

Traditional Dwellings

Living in rural areas of southern Africa generally means living without the amenities of modern life now common in developed nations. Rural homes are usually simple structures, built using cement blocks and corrugated steel roofs, or using traditional techniques and materials such as mud, wood, grass, and dung. Every

Kavango men catch fish in a net. Fishing is an important part of the local economies of villages and towns along rivers.

These homes in a Zulu village are made of sticks and grass. The Zulu have been using these building materials for generations.

ethnic group builds its traditional houses with the natural materials found in the environment in which they live. Among the Zulu, for example, traditional homebuilding materials include sticks and grass. The book, *Cultural Atlas of Africa,* describes how traditional Zulu homes are made. "The framework of Zulu houses was an arrangement of two sets of semi-circular hoops, arranged at right angles to one another, and tied where they intersected. This framework was covered first with matting and then with thick layers of grass thatch."[4]

Ethnic groups like the Zulu, who emphasize agriculture, are not the only groups who continue to build their homes from traditional materials. The Sambyu people, who traditionally practice a mixed economy of fishing, agriculture, and herding along the banks of the Okavango River in Angola and neighboring Namibia, make traditional huts of the canes, grasses, and mud that are found along the river. Anthropologists Gordon D. Gibson, Thomas J. Larson, and Cecilia R. McGurk describe how these huts are built.

There are two types of huts today, circular and rectangular. The rectangular house varies in plan from approximately 3 m. × 3 m. to 5 m. × 8 m. and is usually divided into three or four rooms. . . .

The round hut has an average diameter of 4 m. The frame for the conical roofs is usually made on the ground and set on top of the circular wall after it is completed.

Grass, either tied in bundles or loose, is sewed to thatch the roofs of both types of houses. Canes are placed across each layer of grass and then covered with more grass. . . .

On the inside the walls are plastered with mud, and occasionally the outsides are also plastered, but usually the structural framework is visible from the outside.[5]

According to the *South Africa Survey 1999/2000*, 25 percent of people living in the nation of South Africa continue to inhabit traditional homes such as these, and the percentage is higher for other countries in the region.

Traditional homes of wood, mud, and grass generally do not have modern amenities such as electricity, running water, or sanitation. Even many modern rural homes do not feature such luxuries. Water usually comes from sources away from the home, such as outside pumps, or rivers, streams, and dams. And most households still use pit toilets for sanitation, kerosene lamps for lighting, and fires for cooking.

But while these rural lifestyles may seem simple by Western standards, few lifestyles could be considered more primitive than those of southern Africa's remaining hunter-gatherers.

Hunting and Gathering Lifestyle

A small percentage of rural southern Africans continue to make their living as their ancestors did hundreds, and even thousands, of years ago: hunting wild animals and gathering wild plant foods. The San Bushmen in Botswana and related tribes such as the !Kung hunt wild animals and gather wild plant foods in the nearly uninhabitable plains of the Kalihari Desert of Botswana, Namibia, Angola, and South Africa. Traditionally nomadic—moving in small, mobile groups—a small percentage of the San Bushmen are thought to continue to follow herds of animals and the fruiting cycles of edible plants just as their ancestors did. Taking advantage of their knowledge of the plants and animals of the bush helps them make a living from the harsh desert environment.

The San Bushmen are believed to be descendants of the oldest residents of southern Africa, speakers of the Khoisan language family who are thought to have migrated to the region from eastern Africa. It is estimated that approximately fifty-five thousand San Bushmen and related ethnic groups live in southern Africa, committed in varying degrees to the hunting and gathering lifestyle. According to anthropologist Jiro Tanaka in his book *The San: Hunter-Gatherers of the Kalahari*, the Northern San of Botswana are more exclusively hunter-gatherers than the Southern San. Overall, however, the percentage of San who continue to practice these traditions is diminishing. Tanaka quotes a study by R.B. Lee, another anthropologist, that concludes:

From the turn of the century, when perhaps 60 percent of the San were

San Bushmen have been hunters for centuries. Few San Bushmen tribes are still nomadic, following wild herds as their main food source.

storing food and tools, and for shelter during infrequent poor weather. Most of the San's traditional lifestyles are spent outside: the men hunting, the women gathering plants, and the children practicing these activities in their play.

Today most San Bushmen and related peoples live in extreme poverty in small villages, learning to farm and care for domestic animals. However, many continue to use the tremendous ingenuity of their traditional ways of hunting and gathering to eke out a living in one of the most unfriendly environments on earth.

Migrant Mine Laborers

Ethnic groups from rural areas also flock to the many gold, diamond, or bulk ore mines of the region, crossing regional and national boundaries in their search for work. Mining income generated by migrant workers is the financial glue that holds together many families in dozens of ethnic groups, particularly the Sotho and Tswana. In many communities throughout the region, at least one family member from each household must leave home to find work, often going to the mines of South Africa, Botswana, Namibia, Swaziland, or Zimbabwe to earn the income necessary to support a family. This kind of

full-time hunters and gatherers, this proportion has steadily dropped until the present, when less than 5 percent of the San simply hunt and gather for a living. However, it is interesting that in every San community, even the most acculturated ones, wild plant foods and game continue to play an important if not primary role in subsistence.[6]

As a nomadic people in a hot, dry region, the traditional houses of the San Bushmen are simply built, well-ventilated structures of sticks loosely thatched with grass and leaves. Houses are used for sleeping, occasional privacy needs, for

migrant mining lifestyle, in which as much as 10 percent of the working population participates, is unique to southern Africa.

Migrant mining culture is exclusively male. Miners travel long distances to work in the mines and live together for months at a time in dormitories. Often banding together by ethnicity and tribal language, they live together, work together, and spend their leisure time with other migrants. Many cultural institutions have grown out of this mining culture, including stomp-dancing groups whose dancing is based on the rhythms established while performing specific types of mining work.

Life for the miners, in this overwhelmingly male culture, is hazardous. Many miners are killed and injured each year in work-related accidents. And when the men are not in the mines, the migrant lifestyle provides additional deadly hazards. Alcoholism is rampant, and so is the spread of disease. AIDS (acquired immunodeficiency syndrome), resulting from unprotected sex with prostitutes, ravages mining populations. And when miners return home a few times each year for holidays,

Miners take a lunch break in a diamond mine in South Africa.

Racial Divisions in Southern Africa

Modern southern African cities tend to be highly segregated, or divided, by race and tribe as well as by income level. The laws of apartheid, which means apartness in Afrikaans (the language of the white Dutch settlers of southern Africa), ensured that in every aspect of life, different ethnicities were kept separate in the postcolonial era. And while these laws have changed, housing, employment, and many other aspects of life continue to be segregated by race throughout the region.

In the nation of South Africa, laws enforcing segregation created a divided society that persists even after apartheid was banished in the early 1990s. A study of East London, South Africa, called *Townsmen or Tribesmen: Conservatism and the Process of Urbanization in a South African City*, by historian Philip Mayer, illustrates how apartheid laws created and enforced segregation.

"In East London . . . the non-White town consists of 'The Locations' (Native locations) set apart by law and custom from the White residential and business areas. In the locations more than fifty thousand people jostle together, some in decent houses or cottages but most in shacks or hovels, and from here most of the able-bodied go forth every morning to do their day's wage earning in White East London. The rest of the non-White population lives scattered about the White areas, in domestic servants quarters on White employers' premises.

White East London . . . is a modern industrial and commercial centre, a considerable seaport and a holiday resort. Outside the business centre its residential suburbs are strung out for several miles along the hills, the river banks and the sandy coastline. In this White world the Black person is allotted and accepts certain roles, above all the role of employee. The main reason why country-born Xhosa come to East London in the first place is to work for or under White East Londoners—as factory hands, general labourers, railway and harbour workers, domestic servants, shops' messengers—and earn wages which will supplement the scanty living they make in the countryside, or perhaps provide their sole means of support.

The migrant is not only permitted but compelled to participate in the White-

they often bring HIV, the virus that causes AIDS, back to their families and villages.

Mining is disruptive to miners' families and communities in other ways as well. The absence of fathers and other male figureheads creates a void of cultural influence in the community and interrupts important cultural rituals. In some cultures, if fathers are not home to participate in their children's initiation ceremonies, the ceremonies might not take place at all, and important traditions and cultural iden-

dominated world. Under present regulations, if he fails to get himself employment in the East London areas the authorities can return him from there to the country."

Since the first multiracial government was elected in 1994, the government of the Republic of South Africa has used the legal system to try to undo years of such blatant discrimination. According to a 2002 article in the *Los Angeles Times* entitled "South African Whites Say Deck Is Stacked Against Them,"

"Under the former system of apartheid, blacks, who make up 77% of the country's population of 43 million, were relegated to menial and labor-intensive jobs, subjected to legalized racial oppression and denied citizenship. Indians and so-called 'coloreds,' or people of mixed race, were placed on a higher rung than blacks but were still considered inferior to whites, who make up about 10.5% of the population.

Today, the Employment Equity Act of 1998 seeks to achieve racial equity in the workplace by demanding that all employers with 50 or more workers undertake measures to promote equal opportunity for people from previously disadvantaged communities."

Unfortunately, this attempt to right wrongs, also known as affirmative action, has alienated many Afrikaners, South Africans of Dutch descent, many of whom are blue-collar workers struggling to move up in the world. The *Los Angeles Times* article quotes Koos Malan, an Afrikaner scholar and spokesman, who sums up the Afrikaner attitude.

"An increasing feeling of isolation has led thousands of Afrikaners to emigrate since 1994 and caused others to insulate themselves within society.

Last year, a survey . . . found that Afrikaners were more likely than any other group to identify race discrimination, and specifically affirmative action policies, as the key issue holding them back in life."

Clearly the attempt to create more racial equality in South Africa is not a painless process, and it will be some time before South Africans of all races can look upon each other as equals in a unified nation.

tities are thus lost. Nonetheless, despite the dangers and disadvantages of the work, thousands of southern Africans, from Namibia to Lesotho and Mozambique, continue to migrate to the mines in a steady stream.

Urban Life

Even in urban areas the people of southern Africa use ingenuity to take advantage of mixed economic opportunities. Often living in ethnic enclaves, or neighborhoods of people from the same tribe, urban dwellers work together to make a living. In cities across the region the population is sharply divided between those who can make an adequate living and those who cannot, those who are rich and those who are poor. Every southern African city includes neighborhoods of each: urban centers with skyscrapers, suburbs with wealthy and middle-class homes, and makeshift informal shantytowns with no amenities. Everywhere in southern Africa, city folk mix in a strange stew of ethnicities, languages, and economic levels.

Wealthy neighborhoods in southern Africa are much like those in North America and are largely occupied by whites and the few Indian, African, and mixed-race residents who can afford to live in these areas. Brick houses line well-tended streets. Houses have electricity, and fresh water is piped in while sewage is piped out. Cars stand in every driveway. Only a very small percentage of southern Africans can afford such luxury, however, and despite the gains blacks and other races have made since the end of apartheid laws which kept races separate up to the early 1990s, most wealthy southern Africans are white. The majority of urban dwellers are part of a growing middle class, living modest lives in the urban townships and suburbs surrounding the cities.

A shantytown in a southern African city has very little in the way of modern amenities such as electricity and clean running water.

Indians of South Africa

Indians from South Asia make up about 3 percent of the southern African population today, mostly living in the KwaZulu-Natal region of South Africa. Indians came to the region in two groups: as indentured servants, whose passage to South Africa was paid for by others in exchange for free labor; and as free Indians, entrepreneurs who paid for their own passage. These groups were generally of different castes, or classes, free Indians being generally more wealthy and educated and of a higher class. Free Indians worked as owners of small businesses and as professionals, while indentured Indians often worked as laborers. The majority of Indians in southern Africa today are descendants of indentured laborers.

In India the wealthy and poor castes of Indians had different roles and privileges in society. In the racist atmosphere of South Africa, however, Indians found that caste and class did not matter: All Indians were the victims of discriminatory laws. Surendra Bhana and Bridglal Pachai, editors of the book *A Documentary History of Indian South Africans*, published a 1978 document of the South African Indian Council, a governmental advisory council with no lawmaking power, which shows a little of South Africa's historical discrimination against Indians.

"It is recorded that the year 1860 saw the landing of the first batch of Indians at Port Natal under contract to serve their white masters in tending, nurturing and extending the cane-fields in Natal. This was the primary purpose of the labour contract and if the Indians were employed in other forms of servitude, it was because of the dearth of labour and the recognition of the Indian's wide range of adaptability. . . .

The indentured Indian had the right to exercise one of two options: either to return to India on a free passage after his contract had expired or to remain in Natal as a citizen enjoying the rights and privileges of white Natalians. But this solemn assurance was never at any rate carried out and the disillusionment was complete when measures were taken to repatriate the Indians and their descendants. The political struggles that ensued before and after the Act of Union [when South Africa became a nation] do not require repetition as the story of the Indian people is contained in the annals of South African history. That story is one of struggles against the restrictions imposed on them, their rejection by the whites of Natal, their inferior social and political status and, above all, what the United Nations proclaims, the deprivation of fundamental human rights. It is the latter that has become a matter of the gravest contention and . . . has awakened the conscience of the world to the evils of racial segregation."

The urban middle class in southern Africa includes people of all ethnicities and races. Employed as civil servants and in business and trade, the middle class lives in neighborhoods of apartments, row houses, small houses, or in traditional structures such as huts on the edges of the suburbs. While most of these urban middle-class homes have electricity and water piped in, some still access clean water at taps outside, light their homes with kerosene lamps or candles, and use pit toilets for sanitation. Few own cars; instead, they use public transportation, bicycles, and walking to get around. But life could be worse for the middle class. For the urban poor that crowd the edges of every southern African city, electricity, clean water, sanitation, and even land ownership are ill-afforded luxuries.

Nearly 20 percent of urban dwellers in South Africa live in abject poverty. These people inhabit informal squatter settlements, unofficial shantytowns that have sprung up near urban centers all over southern Africa. Housing here consists mostly of shacks made of scrap wood, metal, cardboard, and plastic—materials from which poor migrants can build a shelter. These settlements have very limited access to electricity, clean water, or sanitation, and even public water taps and pit toilets may be some distance from homes. Despite the fact that most urban dwellers have come to the city to search for work, unemployment in squatter settlements can be as high as 50 percent.

Those who do find work labor in crafts or trade, hire on as domestic servants, or perform manual labor at low wages. Those who do not find work often turn to crime. The crime rate of some southern African cities is startlingly high. In South Africa, for example, the rate of gun violence is the fourth highest in the world, just behind third-ranked United States. And the rate of robbery and violent theft is among the highest in the world. Yet, despite the unique problems of living in cities, people continue to flock to urban areas in southern Africa to search for work, leaving behind their farms and flocks in rural areas.

Changing Lifestyles

The lifestyles of southern Africans today are both different and the same as those of their ancestors. Many ethnic groups continue to live in the same types of homes as their forefathers, making a living in much the same way, be it through agriculture or through a mixed economy of herding and farming. The majority of southern Africans continue to live without modern amenities such as electricity and running water.

But the legacy of the colonial and apartheid eras, as well as the challenges of modern African economies, have changed the lifestyles of southern Africans dramatically. Migrant labor has become a necessity for families in almost every nation in the region, and practicing a mixed economy, making a living in more than one way with some outside form of income, has become a modern way of life.

Chapter 2

Indigenous Kingdoms of Southern Africa

Southern Africa has been the home of complex indigenous states for over a thousand years. While European-centered histories of Africa once taught that southern Africa was largely uninhabited before the arrival of Europeans, nothing could be further from the truth. The region, which was home to scattered Khoisan-speaking hunter-gatherers and pastoralists before the Christian era, A.D. 0, hosted numerous cultures, cities, and states long before the arrival of Europeans in the fifteenth and seventeenth centuries. These states, with a variety of distinct lifestyles, were inhabited by the ancestors of the people who live in southern Africa today, and their ways of life greatly influenced the cultures of modern-day southern Africans. Kingdoms which thrived on cattle-herding, mining, and trade used the natural resources of the region to develop cultural traditions and lifestyles which are as relevant today as they were hundreds of years ago. And in looking at these early states it is possible to see the origins of modern southern Africa.

The Rise of Southern African States

The indigenous cultures of southern Africa began to develop into states around the end of the first millennium, A.D. 900 to 1000, a period often called the Late Iron Age by archeologists and historians due to humans' first recorded use of iron tools. Before that time, southern African cultures were organized into small chiefdoms, generally clans of related people led by chiefs or elders, and allegiance to these leaders changed frequently. If a group of people did not like the leadership of their chief, they would simply split off from the clan and migrate elsewhere to set up their homes. Around the tenth century, however, this leadership model began to change.

Around A.D. 1000, near the Limpopo River there arose several powerful states and kingdoms in which power and leadership were retained for as long as several centuries. These kingdoms grew from the consolidation, or grouping together, of

Rewriting the History of Southern Africa

Long before the advent of the twentieth-century racist apartheid government in the Republic of South Africa, whites of the region came to believe a popular myth about the settling of the region. According to historian Kevin Shillington in his book *History of Africa*, whites of the region were taught to believe

"that black Bantu-speaking, iron-working farmers only crossed the Limpopo River into southern Africa during the seventeenth century, that is, about the same time as white settlers first arrived in South Africa. According to this tradition, in the seventeenth and eighteenth centuries, white settlers entered an 'empty land', peopled only by a few scattered Khoikhoi pastoralists and San hunters. . . . They used [this belief] as justification for claiming ownership over a vast majority of the land in the country. . . ."

In reality, nothing could have been further from the truth. According to historians who study prehistory through archeological and linguistic, or language, data, Bantu-speaking tribesmen came to southern Africa as early as the first century A.D., and were well established by A.D. 400.

One of the reasons for this misconception about southern African history was that, for many years, the racist apartheid government of the Republic of South Africa suppressed the study of southern African history. According to a United Nations–sponsored *General History of Africa*, volume 4, "Because of apartheid, the history of the black peoples south of the Limpopo [River] has been studied less than that of other African populations."

The study recounts the reason for this lack of study: the refusal of historians and publishers of the region to examine or pub-

several smaller chiefdoms for protection or economic and trade advantage. Historian Kevin Shillington, author of several histories of Africa, writes of the economy of this period.

In general the Later Iron Age was a period of great economic, social and political development. As people

learnt to make the most of their local environment, agricultural and fishing techniques were improved and mining and manufacturing skills further developed, . . . there was an increasing emphasis upon cattle-keeping as people brought the drier grasslands into greater use. Certain communities specialized in mining, metal

lish any historical record of the region that did not emphasize white history. Publishers and historians would not even acknowledge historical records written by eyewitnesses of other nations, such as the Portuguese, or nonwritten historical records, such as oral histories. The UN report states that

"White historians in South Africa have refused the aid of such sciences as archaeology, anthropology and linguistics. Even more serious is the fact that the official historians of the country of apartheid draw from the archives materials which relates only to the whites, deliberately putting aside documents referring to African peoples."

Fortunately, the study of history in southern Africa opened up with the fall of the apartheid government in South Africa in the early 1990s, paving the way for the publishing of more accurate and inclusive histories of the region.

A Bantu chief in tribal headdress is pictured in a painting from the late 1800s.

manufacture, food production or hunting. All of this regional specialization helped promote inter-regional trade. . . . With the development of Later Iron Age specializations and population growth people organized into larger political units and there was a rise in the power and importance of territorial chiefs.[7]

These territorial chiefs retained their power and kept their kingdoms together through a number of means: through military might, economic rewards, and religious or ideological beliefs. In the new, more stable states that grew through such leadership, the first southern African cities were built and the region's first complex system of trade, industry, and government developed.

Agro-Pastoralist Communities

The first states in southern Africa were probably cattle-keeping states led by powerful chiefs who owned vast herds. South of the Zambezi River, on the open grasslands of the region known as the veld, cattle-keeping became a major source of wealth and power. While most cattle-keeping kingdoms had mixed economies, practicing agriculture to some degree as well as pastoralism, cattle were the main source of wealth.

Cattle-keeping kingdoms were stable and strong because cattle were a reliable source of food—as producers of milk most often, and more rarely meat—in a region often beset by drought. Cattle were also a means to accumulate wealth and power. Cattle could be traded with other communities for food and iron tools. Cattle could also be loaned to client herders, people too poor to own cattle who herded the animals in exchange for the use of the cattle's milk. Cattle could even be used as *lobola*, or bridewealth gifts given to a family in exchange for the right to marry a daughter. Since those with more cattle had more *lobola* to afford more wives—along with

the agricultural labor and children they eventually provided—they had many means to become rich and powerful in their communities. According to historian Martin Hall, livestock were important both as wealth and for the social positions they enabled their owners to possess.

Livestock could accumulate, granting their owners an increased degree of protection for the vagaries of agricultural production. The importance of domestic animals is attested by the innumerable stone byres [cattle pens] of the high grassland regions of southern Africa, by the place of livestock in the economies of communities that have been described ethnog-

A young herder in Botswana oversees his employer's cattle. Cattle are an important food source and a sign of wealth.

raphically, and, to the west, by the frequent raids that Khoikhoi carried out on their neighbours in order to increase their stock holdings. Apart from their social importance, domestic animals provided hides for clothing, shields and shelter, bone for artifacts, and blood, milk, and meat. . . .

Livestock were of central importance in the transactions in Khoikhoi society that bound people together in networks of mutual obligation. Cattle and sheep played an extremely important role in Khoikhoi society and, by extension, in Khoikhoi history. Possession of livestock was the main criterion by which Khoikhoi were distinguished from hunters, and rich Khoikhoi tribes from poor. Within each tribe, livestock was important in almost every realm of life: the economic, aesthetic, political and social.[8]

Among the Khoikhoi, Khoisan speakers in the Cape region of South Africa, ownership of cattle came to be associated with social positions which were evident in many aspects of life, such as the placement of the homes within a community settlement. In addition, according to a United Nations–sponsored history of Africa, the accumulation of individual and clan wealth in the form of cattle led to the development of chieftaincies. "Politically, the Khoikhoi were divided into sets of clans and when the cattle stock waxed [grew], they formed larger politi-

cal units, under the leadership of hereditary chiefs."[9]

Adding to the image of the Khoikhoi power structure, historian Martin Hall writes,

> The historically known Khoikhoi of the western subcontinent clearly had a form of social organization which can be seen as an example of the chiefdom. Each polity had leaders who inherited their power from their fathers. These chiefdoms were often ranked, with some owning allegiance to more powerful groups, often located a considerable distance away. But chiefs only held power by consent of their councils of leading followers.[10]

Thus, among these early Khoikhoi chiefdoms, power was not permanent and hereditary but rather fluid and based on personal wealth and power.

The development of chieftaincies led to the development of larger states. Among the Sotho-Tswana, for example, in the central region of the southern African highveld, the ancestors of the modern-day Sotho-Tswana people built powerful cattle-keeping kingdoms led by strong chiefs who passed power down over generations. The most powerful Sotho-Tswana leaders built large settlements, and by the end of the eighteenth century, one such kingdom, known as the Tlhaping, had a capital city of between fifteen and twenty thousand people. These settlements were sophisticated in structure. According to historian Kevin Shillington, in his book *A History of Southern Africa,*

> The usual pattern for these settlements was a large centralized town, surrounded by agricultural fields. Beyond these lay extensive grazing lands for their cattle. The towns themselves were divided into wards. Each ward was usually made up of a group of related families. The whole settlement was ruled over by a chief. He was head of the senior ward and probably the owner of the most cattle. . . . A large group of related settlements might consider themselves a "nation" (*morafe*).[11]

In addition to keeping cattle and practicing agriculture, these settlements often traded with each other as well as with settlements with other commodities to offer.

Trading Kingdoms

Cattle were not the only commodity traded by kingdoms in southern Africa. Trade was an especially powerful force in developing states along the rivers of southern Africa and along the Indian Ocean coast. Before the eighth century, on the coast of Mozambique between the mouths and on the banks of the Limpopo and Zambezi Rivers, several early kingdoms grew powerful through trade with the Arab ships which plied the waters between Asia and Africa. This area of southern Africa still continues to be involved in trade due to its proximity to coastal and riverside trading routes.

One example of a riverside trading kingdom was a city called Ingombe Ilede, or "the place where cows lie."[12] Ingombe

Settlements along the banks of the Zambezi River like this one continue to benefit from coastal and riverside trading.

Ilede grew up on the Zambezi floodplain between 1400 and 1500. Evidence such as gold, copper, cloth, glass beads, and seashells from burial sites, discovered in 1960, suggests that at least some of the people of Ingombe Ilede accumulated a great deal of wealth through trade. However, according to a United Nations–sponsored history of Africa, historians can do no more than theorize about the role trade played in the lives of Ingombe Ilede's residents.

> The remarkable thing about these burials is that, with the exception of the pottery, almost all the grave furniture consists of artifacts or material obtained by long distance trade. . . . On the face of it, there seems no good reason for a site like Ingombe Ilede to be involved in long-distance trade, for there are no local sources of metal ore [to make objects prized by foreign traders]. The explanation may lie in the abundant salt deposits of the River Lusitu, for cake salt was a highly prized commodity in the Iron Age, one that was bartered extensively at the local level. Control of salt deposits may have brought the Ingombe Ilede people into contact with other communities . . . who would accept salt in exchange for their precious metals, which Ingombe Ilede could in turn barter for imported luxuries obtained from the east-coast trade.[13]

Some historians believe that the community did have a source of copper that attracted distant trade. When this copper source ran dry, these historians speculate that Ingombe Ilede was abandoned. Mining for metals such as copper, iron, and gold had become an essential aspect of trade in many parts of the region and drove the creation of several powerful kingdoms in the region—particularly the kingdom known as Great Zimbabwe.

Gold Mining States

Gold mining in what is now the modern republic of Zimbabwe began in the earliest part of the second millennium, around A.D. 1000, and has continued up to the present. The most famous gold mining kingdom of the Late Iron Age was Great Zimbabwe, the culture for which the modern nation is named and the home of the ancestors of the modern Shona people of Zimbabwe. Today, Zimbabwe continues to be famous for its mining industry.

Gold mining in Great Zimbabwe and the surrounding regions was undertaken mainly by peasants in the winter months between harvesting and planting. The peasants themselves probably kept little of the metal as it was of little use within Great Zimbabwe. Most gold went into the coffers of the empire's leaders to be used for trade. According to historian Martin Hall,

> Nothing is known of the manner by which the metal was collected from rural villages and traded for cloth, beads and other imports. . . . The network of regional *madzimbahwe*

The *Madzimbahwe* of Great Zimbabwe

Great Zimbabwe was named for the dry, mortar-free stone enclosures called *madzimbahwe* built in and around their cities between A.D. 1200 and 1450. The people of Great Zimbabwe developed stone masonry to a fine craft, cutting precise square stones and stacking them up into walls and towers up to ten meters high which may have been for defense.

The stonework may also have had another function. The walls and towers may have had a religious or mystical function in society. Evidence of the mystical function of the stonework can be seen in certain towers, where iconic sculptures of birds of prey have been found alongside towering pedestals. While historians do not yet know with certainty the role these towers and sculptures played in society, historian Martin Hall writes in this book,

The Changing Past: Farmers, Kings and Traders in Southern Africa, 200–1860:

"The symbolism and probable function of the Zimbabwe birds can be understood in terms of Shona [the predominant tribe of Zimbabwe] beliefs. Birds, and particularly eagles, were seen as messengers to and from ancestral spirits and between men and God. . . . The role of the ancestor spirit depended on the importance of the earthly person in whom the spirit had once resided. . . . It is thus probable that the carved birds from Great Zimbabwe were metaphors for the spirits of departed kings."

And thus it was also probable that at least some of the stonework in which these birds were found played a role in the religious beliefs of the people of Great Zimbabwe.

[stone towers] and the size and obvious pre-eminence of Great Zimbabwe indicate a structured and sustained political economy in which the acquisition of wealth by the nobility was assured. This in turn suggests strong control over the distribution of gold, which was after all the main basis for the wealth of the state. Therefore, even though gold mining was clearly an industry at the disposal of many peasant villagers, it would seem probable that the metal was a major part in the tribute payable to the nobility.[14]

Gold and other tribute increased the power of the early Shona chiefs who built their political power by financially rewarding and feeding their supporters and dependents. This wealth and political power led, in turn, to the consolidation of religious power among the Shona leadership. The leaders of Great Zimbabwe were thought to have magical and religious powers, and this gave them even greater control over their people. This tradition of ascribing religious powers to tribal leaders is true even today among many southern African ethnic groups: Many traditional leaders hold great emotional and religious sway over their people.

Religious and Military Empires

Religious power was also used as a unifying force to bring together the disparate ethnic groups in what is now Angola. Beginning as guardians of local rainmaking shrines, regional leaders of the Ndongo, Pende, and Libolo people began gaining power by the early twelfth century, "assuming the positions of chiefs and exacting tribute for their services,"[15] according to historian, Kevin Shillington. Many of these early chiefs were known to have metal-working skills which were new to the region and which may have given them additional powers over the people. Regardless of the source of their power, the guardians of the rainmaking shrines were able to join the Ndongo chiefdoms together into a unified state, ruled over by a single *Ngola a Kiluanje*, or ruler. This unified territory would form the basis of the modern nation of Angola several centuries later.

Religion, trade, and wealth were not the only means leaders had of unifying people and gaining and maintaining power. Power

Tribal leaders assemble for a traditional healing ceremony in the hope of ridding their land of racism.

just as often was gained through military might as through trade, and often was used by southern African kingdoms intent on expanding their territories. The Mutapa state, with its leader Munhumutapa, was one such state. Around 1420, Nyatsimbe Mutota, a local leader from Great Zimbabwe, seceded from that state and established a new state called Mutapa, in the northern part of what is now Zimbabwe. Mutota and his son and successor Matope took advantage of opportunities for trade with the Swahili coast and later the Portuguese to gain the wealth necessary to quickly expand their empire, and they used military might to control their subjects.

The Mfecane and Difaqane

The rulers of Mutapa were not the only, nor the most powerful, leaders to use military might to expand their territory and demand tribute. In the nineteenth century, during a period of intense turmoil, many new states were created through military conquest and were maintained through payments of tribute. This period of turmoil and conquest was known as the *Mfecane*, or crushing, in the Nguni language, and the *Difaqane*, or scattering, in the Sotho-Tswana language. These names were given to this period because as new states were created, scores of older states were crushed and their subjects were sent scattering throughout southern, central, and eastern Africa. The political and ethnic makeup of the entire region was changed dramatically during the *Mfecane/Difaqane*, creat-

ing many of the states and ethnic groups that populate southern Africa today.

The *Mfecane/Difaqane* was set in motion by disruptions both natural and man-made. The natural event was a ten-year drought around 1800 which destroyed the lush crops and grazing lands of the region and caused widespread famine. This famine led to unrest among the people of the region for nearly twenty years as different states competed for scarce grazing and agricultural resources. This human unrest was largely caused by a small group of Nguni speakers who rose up to dominate the entire region: the Zulu.

In 1800 the Zulu were a small group within the Mthethwa kingdom of Nguni speakers. During the famine the three Nguni kingdoms, which had existed in relative peace for centuries, battled each other for the precious resources to feed their people and cattle. When the Mthethwa chief was killed, a regimental leader from a tributary clan, the Zulu, rose up to lead the kingdom. His name was Shaka, and he would go down in history as one of the greatest military leaders Africa has ever known.

Shaka developed new weapons and tactics for warfare and built standing armies of young men both from the Nguni kingdoms and from newly incorporated tribes. He also reorganized the Zulu kingdom along military lines, creating a society controlled by fear which was perpetually at war and which relied on expansion for its prosperity. By the time he was killed in 1828, the Zulu kingdom had expanded to become the largest in southern Africa. Today, those who identify themselves as Zulu comprise the largest ethnic group in the Republic of South Africa.

Along with the famine, the expansion of the Zulu propelled the *Mfecane/Difaqane*. Ethnic groups displaced by the Zulu used the Zulu military methods to conquer other peoples and steal their land. Like the fall of a stack of dominoes, the conflict moved to the north, south, east, and west, claiming victims for thousands of miles and creating untold numbers of refugees. The mayhem of the *Mfecane/Difaqane* led not only to the destruction of states, however, but also to the creation of several new, powerful, and centralized states, some of which remain to this day.

One powerful state created during that time was the BaSotho state of Chief Moshoeshoe, a state which would later form the basis for the modern nation of Lesotho. Fleeing the expanding Zulu kingdom, Moshoeshoe created a new kingdom on a protected plateau northwest of the Drakensburg Mountains. Refugees from many parts of southern Africa fled to Moshoeshoe's kingdom for protection. According to historian Kevin Shillington's book *A History of Southern Africa*, "Moshoeshoe presented a chance for peace and security. People were attracted to his side by his offers of protec-

A Zulu warrior poses for a late 1800s photograph. During the 1800s the Zulu kingdom rose to power under the leadership of Shaka.

tion, his increasing wealth in cattle and his ability to defend his mountain stronghold. Refugees from the surrounding country quickly joined him."[16]

While some ethnic groups broke up and became refugees, some kingdoms fled Shaka's armies as a group, establishing homelands elsewhere by stealing the land of other peoples. One Nguni-speaking group, the Khumalo, wandered as refugees

The Rise of Shaka and the Zulu Kingdom

Shaka, the innovative leader of the Zulu kingdom, changed the nature of warfare in southern Africa, single-handedly setting the stage for the region-wide disruptions known as *Mfecane/Difaqane*. Before Shaka, cattle raids by Nguni-speaking ethnic groups generally aimed to steal cattle and show enough strength to scare other ethnic groups into paying tribute to Nguni leaders. Under Shaka, warfare no longer aimed to scare. Its aim was total destruction of the enemy. According to historian Shillington in his book *A History of Southern Africa,* "The enemy was to be totally destroyed and so never allowed to recover. Armies were defeated, homesteads burned, women and children killed and all enemy livestock captured."

In order to effect this new strategy, Shaka developed a number of military as well as administrative innovations. First, he armed each soldier with a short stabbing spear and a body-length shield for protection from enemy spears. Second, he developed new military tactics. According to Shillington, "Shaka developed the 'cow-horn' formation. While the bulk of his army faced the enemy, regiments were sent out on each side like two great horns. While the 'chest' charged forward in the centre, the 'horns' encircled the enemy and prevented their escape."

Shaka also developed new means of organizing Zulu society along military lines. This reorganization served to direct all the ethnic group's energies and efforts toward warfare and expansion. Men and women were forced to live in segregated military regiments and those who did not show courage were executed. Only men and women who had completed military service were allowed to marry and were finally free to live apart from the regiments.

for nearly twenty years, ultimately setting up their kingdom under the new name of Ndebele, the Nguni word for "Nguni-speaking strangers," in Zimbabwe, where they remain to this day.

The movement of refugees and the setting up of new states during the *Mfecane/ Difaqane* also led to the mixing of cultures. The Swazi nation was an example of such a mixed state. The Swazi, founded by an Nguni leader of the Ngwane kingdom and his son Mswati, fled north, away from the Zulu, and built a new nation through diplomacy, marriage alliances with Sotho chieftains, and conquest. The new Swazi kingdom, which later became the modern nation of Swaziland, took on many Sotho characteristics which remain today, such as the holding of *libandla*, nationwide general meetings to decide matters of importance, and the political importance of the mother of the king, the *Ndlhovukati* (the "Great She-Elephant").

An Influence on the Future

The early states of southern Africa foretold the lifestyles of ethnic groups in the region today and influenced the creation of modern nations. Early states grew in response to the available resources of the area, be it grazing lands for cattle, minerals for mining, or waterways for trade. And the military conquests so common to the region, especially during the *Mfecane/ Difaqane* period of the 1800s, helped consolidate the use of scarce resources and create the concentrated population patterns and ethnic identities found in southern Africa when the Europeans began expanding in the region in the nineteenth century.

Chapter 3

Europeans in Southern Africa

Starting in the sixteenth century, four European nations began to explore southern Africa with an eye to exploiting the resources of the region: Portugal, the Netherlands, Britain, and to a lesser extent, Germany. Each nation sought to carve out a commercial and political niche in a region already busy with indigenous African kingdoms and cultures. These foreigners established relations, both good and bad, with the African cultures of the region, claiming territory and influence over large areas and clashing with both African kingdoms and the other European nations over their rights to territories, resources, and people.

The Europeans explored and colonized southern Africa in different ways, but they all had common interests in the region: commercial and political exploitation. And in order to exploit the resources of southern Africa and gain control over territory, each European nation found different ways to dominate and control the area's many ethnic groups: through military might, by playing groups off against each other, and through legal means.

Commerce and Captives: The Impact of Portuguese Trade

For the Portuguese, who arrived in southern Africa in the 1500s, the region was part of an extensive commercial network that was spread along the coasts of west and east Africa. Through the river systems of Angola in the west and Mozambique in the east, the Portuguese dreamed of linking the two extremities of their African empire. And while this dream was never realized, the Portuguese made a tremendous impact on southern Africa through their commercial exploits.

Ferias and the Slave Trade

The Portuguese commercial and political presence in southern Africa influenced the region both culturally and economically. Portuguese trade, primarily in slaves in Angola and in gold and ivory in Mozambique, changed the nature of both African trade and culture. While there had long been a demand for gold, ivory, and slaves in many African kingdoms, for both the internal African and Arab markets, the scale of trade—especially the slave trade—grew exponentially under the Portuguese. They exported gold, ivory, and slaves to Europe and across the Atlantic. By the late 1600s the port city of Luanda, Angola, was a major slaving station, exporting to Europe more than ten thousand captives a year.

Many slaves were captured in warfare by the *Ngola*, king of the Ndongo people, in exchange for Portuguese protection from the *Ngola*'s enemies. According to historian Kevin Shillington, the effects of the slave trade—especially the wars—on what is now the nation of Angola were devastating to the social, economic, and political systems of Angola.

Wars . . . may not have generally been waged deliberately to produce

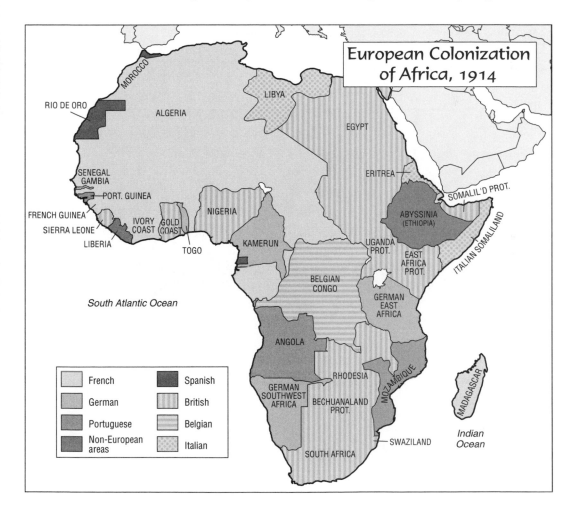

European Colonization of Africa, 1914

MOROCCO
RIO DE ORO
ALGERIA
LIBYA
EGYPT
SENEGAL
GAMBIA
PORT. GUINEA
ERITREA
SOMALIL'D PROT.
FRENCH GUINEA
SIERRA LEONE
LIBERIA
IVORY COAST
GOLD COAST
TOGO
NIGERIA
KAMERUN
ABYSSINIA (ETHIOPIA)
ITALIAN SOMALILAND
UGANDA PROT.
EAST AFRICA PROT.
BELGIAN CONGO
GERMAN EAST AFRICA
South Atlantic Ocean
ANGOLA
RHODESIA
MOZAMBIQUE
MADAGASCAR
GERMAN SOUTHWEST AFRICA
BECHUANALAND PROT.
SWAZILAND
Indian Ocean
SOUTH AFRICA

French
German
Portuguese
Non-European areas
Spanish
British
Belgian
Italian

captives for sale. But the presence of Europeans on the coast offering what appeared to be high prices for captives undoubtedly stimulated warfare. This was especially so in the eighteenth century when Europeans offered guns as their major trading item. It made war more profitable. . . . Whereas previously war might have stopped at the levying of tribute and the taking of some captives, now it became "total"—the total destruction of weaker societies. . . .

In purely economic terms, there was also a serious loss to the produc-

tive potential of the region. . . . [Captives] were sold right out of Africa, and sold for goods which were worth a fraction of what those people might have produced within their own lifetime. In addition, those sold were the young, most productive sector of the population.[17]

Portuguese trade encouraged the European appetite for African products and slaves and created a system for reaching that market. Sailing up the rivers of the southeast coast, the Portuguese established *ferias* among many ethnic groups. *Ferias* were marketplaces where African traders

An illustration shows Europeans inspecting and instructing their southern African slaves.

could bring goods and slaves to be purchased by Portuguese merchants. These marketplaces changed both the economy and society of the region.

For one thing, the presence of the *ferias* changed the nature of tribal society for many ethnic groups. Some southern African ethnic groups gave up their traditional forms of livelihood, such as agriculture or animal husbandry, to become merchants in the new *ferias*, or professional slave traders called *pombeiros*. In addition, the new economy helped develop a large wealthy merchant class in market towns, and these rich merchants often wielded influence they had never known in tribal society. In some cases, wealthy traders replaced traditional tribal leaders and were put in the position of making decisions for the community at large because of their income and social standing.

The Portuguese *ferias* also changed agriculture and the African diet by introducing New-World crops, such as a type of corn called maize from the Americas, to southern Africa. Maize improved the nutrition of many ethnic groups and caused a surge in population in some parts of southern Africa.

The *Prazo* System

The *ferias* and the market systems they encouraged were not the only evidence of Portuguese influence on the economic, social, and political systems of southern African cultures. Along the Zambezi River, Portuguese and mixed-race Afro-Portuguese colonists established a new system of land ownership and taxation in southern Africa called the *prazo* system which greatly expanded the Portuguese influence in the southeast. The *prazo* system began when these colonists and traders took on the status of political chiefs over former tribal land along the Zambezi River. They assumed this status either through conquest or by demanding compensation for some service provided to local rulers. According to a United Nations–sponsored history of Africa, the leaders of the *prazos* had nearly absolute power over their subjects on the *prazeros*. "The big *prazos* were more than private estates. They amounted to areas of jurisdiction in which the estate-owners commonly known as *prazeros* 'had absolute power of justice, waged war, imposed tribute, and were often guilty of great barbarities.'"[18]

The *prazeros* treated their subjects harshly, demanding both labor and taxes for the right to live on land which had often previously been owned by the subjects themselves. The *prazeros* used private armies of paid African subjects to control people, expand territory and trading relations, force labor, and demand payment of tribute.

While the *prazos* did not officially expand Portuguese colonial territory, the Portuguese government encouraged the creation of *prazos*, believing them to be an example of private enterprise which would attract more Portuguese immigrants to southern Africa and thereby increase the Portuguese presence in the region.

Boers: The Impact of Dutch Immigrants

Portugal was not the only nation to try to attract immigrants to southern Africa. Through a commercial venture called the Dutch East India Company, Holland sought to establish territories in southern Africa by encouraging landless peasants to settle there and expand Dutch influence in the region.

In the late fifteenth century the Dutch East India Company established a resupply station on the Cape of Good Hope, a place to replenish the food and water of ships bound for India. Dutch settlers were brought in to grow vegetables and fruits and raise beef for the passing ships. These settlers, often poor, landless peasants in Holland, were given land and slaves from west Africa, Madagascar, and Indonesia to work their farms. The immigrants called themselves Boers, the Dutch word for farmer. Over time the Boers became culturally very different from their relations in Holland, eventually going so far as developing a new language with Dutch and African influences, called Afrikaans, and calling themselves Afrikaners.

But the Boers changed more than their own culture in southern Africa. They changed the indigenous cultures, the economies, political systems, and territorial boundaries of their adopted homeland. One way the Boers changed the territorial makeup of the region was through expansion. As the population of the Cape increased—by the late 1700s there were twenty-one thousand Boers and twenty-five thousand slaves—Boer settlers moved inland to the north, west, and east in search of grazing and agricultural land. This expansion brought the Boers into conflict with the Khoi and Xhosa, pastoral ethnic groups who traditionally used the Cape as grazing land for their cattle, as well as other ethnic groups with whom they came into contact.

The Boers' conflicts with indigenous groups had the effect of destroying some of the indigenous cultures with whom they came into contact. While the Bantu-speaking Xhosa resisted Boer pressures and remained strong culturally, many Khoi, Khoisan-speaking pastoralists, lost their cattle and livelihoods and were forced to work for the Boers at extremely low-paying jobs as animal herders and hunters. This had the effect of destroying the cultural integrity of many Khoi groups as they became essentially landless workers removed from their traditional culture and lifestyle. Some fled to the north, establishing new societies called the Griqua, Kora, and Nama, which captured, bred, and sold cattle on the frontier. Today the Khoi as an ethnic group do not exist, and their descendants, often of mixed-race ancestry and Afrikaans names, identify themselves as members of the Nama or other ethnic groups.

Despite their influence on many African ethnic groups, the Boers' conflicts were not limited to indigenous Africans. The Boers' most defining battles, the first movements for the Boers' Afrikaner

The Afrikaners—White Tribe of South Africa?

The Afrikaners, Africans of Dutch descent, have lived in southern Africa for hundreds of years, first arriving in the late fifteenth century. Like most Americans whose ancestors immigrated to North America, Afrikaners have established deep roots in the region, have owned homes and farms for generations, and know southern Africa as their only home. And, like many Americans who live on land which was formerly the home of Native American Indian tribes, many Afrikaners also live on former tribal land.

Some Afrikaners, in fact, identify themselves as Africa's "white tribe." Marq de Villiers, seventh-generation South African and author of *White Tribe Dreaming,* documents the development of a unique Afrikaner culture among the trekboers, Boers who moved away from the relatively civilized areas of the Cape to the inland frontiers.

"On the frontier, among the trekboers, things were very different [than on the Cape]. Their connections to European culture were tenuous and increasingly irrelevant. Company officials and visitors to the interior routinely expressed alarm at the rapidity with which the frontiersmen were abandoning everything 'European.' . . . There were occasional schemes floated to save them from themselves. . . .

But these . . . schemes . . . entirely missed the point, which was that the trekboers had become Africans. Their economy was African. Their loyalties were to the place in which they found themselves, their dreams and songs were of the blue horizons of the north, their art, such as it was, invoked the landscape and their cattle, their hopes were for escape from the dead hand of the Company and the deadly predations of the San and Xhosa cattle raiders. Their houses were usually a few rooms with mud walls and a reed mat for a front door. Only their Bibles gave them a thin, tenuous link with literacy and the larger ideas of the outside world.

On the fringes of the northern and north-western frontiers, the trekboers often lived in the open, or in their wagons. . . . They learned from the Khoikhoi matters of survival in the veld that would become essential items of frontier lore. . . . But generally the trekboers didn't 'go native' in the traditional sense of adopting native culture. Instead, they created their own African culture."

A group of Boers poses with their black servants along the trail during the massive 1835–1840s migration inland known as the Great Trek.

nationalist identity, were fought with an- other European power: the British, who gained control of the Cape Colony in 1795.

When the British acquired the Cape Colony as part of their worldwide naval expansion after the French Revolutionary Wars, they imposed many aspects of British culture on the Dutch Boers. Not surprisingly, the Boers, who by then had been in southern Africa for about two hundred years, resented this British intru- sion. Dissatisfied with British bans on slavery, fair labor laws which regulated the Boers' traditional cruel treatment of

workers, British taxes, and English- language education in schools and courts, Boers, calling themselves Afrikaners, be- gan moving inland in what has come to be known as the Great Trek. This nineteenth century expansion of the Afrikaners com- pletely changed the political and territorial makeup of the region by establishing the first permanent white settlements in the in- terior veld. First settling on land depopu- lated by the *Mfecane/Difaqane*, and later taking the land of ethnic groups such as the Sotho, Ndebele, and Zulu, the Afrikan- ers established what were to become the first independent Afrikaner republics, the

Orange Free State and the South African Republic, also known as the Transvaal.

It was in these newly independent republics, and in the larger Union of South Africa which grew out of them, that the Afrikaners most profoundly affected African life. The Afrikaners developed laws which codified their racist beliefs, laws which later became the notoriously systematized racism known as apartheid. According to a United Nations–sponsored history of Africa, exploitation was built into these early Afrikaner laws.

> Exploitation was built into the citizenship, labour, and other laws enacted by the Boers. The Transvaal [now a region of South Africa] constitution, for instance, rejected any notions of equality between black and white. To rule out any possibility of effective African resistance, the [African] peoples were prohibited from possessing firearms or horses and they were forced to carry passes supplied by their employers or government officials at all times. Each farmer was entitled to keep a number of African families on his farm, who supplied him with regular free labour.[19]

It would be more than a hundred years before all traces of these laws would be wiped from the records of South Africa and other nations of the region. But even today, evidence of the inequality created by apartheid is evident in the clear economic divisions between whites and blacks in southern African society.

German Farmers in Southern Africa

Like the Dutch, Germany's official though brief hold on southern Africa, between 1860 and 1914, was remarkable in its cruel treatment of the indigenous ethnic groups. The German presence in southwest Africa—now Namibia—was also similar to that of the Dutch in the region in that the African territory was originally seen as a land of opportunity for landless German peasants.

In the late 1800s Germany encouraged immigrants to move to southwest Africa to solidify its claim to Namibian territory. In response to this call, thousands of German immigrants flocked to the newly declared German protectorate after 1884, seeking land and opportunity. What they found was scant arable land (most of Namibia is desert), a great deal of land owned by wealthy mining interests, and ethnic groups who did not want to work for the Germans.

In order to force local ethnic groups to work on German farms, the German government created extremely repressive and cruel laws. According to German law, the Nama and Herero pastoralists who occupied the central highveld, and the Ovambo agriculturalists who occupied the northernmost segment of Namibia, were second-class citizens. The Germans encouraged fighting among the Nama and Herero, playing them off against each other and ultimately stealing the land and livelihoods of both groups. Their land was given to German immigrants, and their livelihoods

The Beginning of the End of Apartheid: The Soweto Uprising

One of the most egregious aspects of apartheid was education. Throughout South Africa, black children were educated in Afrikaans, the language of the Afrikaners, despite the fact that few, if any, children in many areas of South Africa spoke Afrikaans. In 1976 South African schoolchildren rose up in a giant wave of protests against the use of Afrikaans in schools. Historian J.D. Omer-Cooper describes the uprising in his book, *History of Southern Africa.*

"In June 1976 schoolchildren throughout Soweto [a slum outside of Johannesburg], staged a massive demonstration against the use of Afrikaans as a medium of instruction. The police used force to disperse the demonstration and it developed into bitter and violent rioting that spread from Soweto to other towns around the Rand and Pretoria and then out of the Transvaal to Natal and the Cape. As the wave of violence spread, moreover, Coloured and Indian youths took part as well as Africans. The riots were far and away the largest outbreaks of racial violence that South Africa had ever seen. Unlike earlier disturbances, moreover, the insurgents did not quickly yield, even to the most drastic use of force. Time and again unarmed youths charged the police through a hail of bullets, displaying a reckless bravery born out of the depths of their bitterness and frustration. No sooner would the upheavals appear to be suppressed than they would flare up again and this continued through the whole of the rest of the year. Even then the relative peace which followed merely masked continuing simmering violence always on the verge of bursting forth again.

In the effort to suppress the upheaval the security forces killed large numbers of young blacks. Hundreds of arrests were made and these were followed by suspiciously large numbers of 'suicides' and unexplained deaths of persons held in police custody. In response large numbers of black youths fled the townships and escaped across South Africa's borders into Botswana or Swaziland. Many of them proved eager recruits for the guerrilla forces of the liberation movements."

destroyed by laws such as bans on cattle ownership and the removal of traditional chiefs. After the Herero and Nama were forced onto small reserves much like the reservations set aside for Native Americans in the United States, many Herero fled to the Kalihari Desert. By the time the German colonization of Namibia had ended, 90 percent of the Herero had perished or fled.

The Ovambo agriculturalists did not disappear in such large numbers as the

Herero, but like the two pastoral groups, they also lost their land and livelihood under German rule. The Ovambo ultimately were forced to work for brutal German farmers and in mines to make a living.

The Germans remained in control of Namibia until after World War I, when Germany's defeat allowed Namibia to be annexed by South Africa under a mandate of the League of Nations, the predecessor of the United Nations. The ethnic groups of Namibia, however, were dramatically and permanently changed by German rule.

The British: Mining for Economic and Political Domination

Like the Germans, the British came into southern Africa much later than the Dutch and Portuguese, but had a great impact on the region in a relatively short period of time. The British gained the Cape Colony in southern Africa at the end of the eighteenth century and valued it as a strategic military outpost. Then, gold and diamonds were discovered in the area, and the British view of the region changed forever.

In 1867, near the confluence of the Orange and Vaal Rivers in an area claimed by several different ethnic groups as well as by the Boers, a Griqua herdsman found one of the largest diamonds ever discovered. Word spread, and prospectors, both white and black, flocked to the region.

Under German rule in the late 1800s the Nama and Herero people, such as the Herero woman pictured, were made second-class citizens in their own homeland.

Historian J.D. Omer-Cooper estimates that by 1871 there were around twenty to twenty-five thousand whites and forty to fifty thousand blacks working in the diamond fields.

In addition to diamond mining, large veins of gold were discovered in 1886 on the southern African highveld, in a region called the Witwatersrand, at the location of what is now the city of Johannesburg. This discovery spurred the British to embark on further exploration for gold in

The Creation of the De Beers Diamond Monopoly

Diamond mining, in the early days of the southern African mineral revolution, was conducted by individual, independent claim owners and the mostly African ethnic groups who worked for them. Living conditions of those who mined the claims were terrible, and working conditions worse. According to historian Kevin Shillington's book *A History of Southern Africa,*

"As the mines got deeper, problems increased. The roadways across the mines collapsed, filling in many claims and killing numbers of workers. As the claims were cleared of falling debris, they acted like huge wells and began to fill with water. By the mid-1870's, it was no longer possible for individual diggers to employ a handful of labourers to work a claim with any real hope of profit. More and more capital was needed. Huge wooden hoists were erected around the Kimberley

mine, with wire ropes running down to the claims at the bottom. Thus hundreds of wire ropes stretched down into the open mine like a giant spider's web connecting each working claim to the surface. Buckets hauled up earth and ferried workers up and down. At first horses were used for turning the wheels which worked the hoists, but in the late 1870's, as the mines got deeper, steam engines were introduced."

One of the first steam engines was brought in by Cecil Rhodes, a British man who saw that the only way diamond mining could be expanded was to create a larger-scale operation. Rhodes's engine pumped out water-sodden diggings, and brought him enough money that he began to purchase diamond claims of his own.

Rhodes was unhappy with competition in the diamond fields. With backing

Bechuanaland (now Botswana) and Rhodesia (now Zimbabwe).

Britain, like other nations in the region, was interested in exploiting and controlling the new mineral resources. Using a cunning mixture of diplomacy, military force, trickery, and economic incentives, Britain, who had no legal claim to the mineral-rich areas at all, gained access to the diamond fields, known as the Kimber-

ley mines, and later to the gold fields of the region. Britain sought control over southern Africa's mineral resources by alternately seeking to unify the various states of the region under British domination, militarily attacking those who would not join the union voluntarily, and tricking native peoples out of their territories. British representatives also played Boer and African ethnic groups off against each

from the powerful English Rothschild family, he took over and joined forces with rival diamond miner, Englishman Barney Barnato. Together they formed De Beers Consolidated, which today is the largest producer of diamonds in the world.

While consolidation was good for Rhodes's business, it wreaked havoc with black diamond miners. According to historian J.D. Omer-Cooper's book *History of Southern Africa*, work conditions at the diamond mines went from bad to worse.

"The amalgamation of the diamond mines not only allowed control of the world market in the interests of the diamond producers, it also brought about an extreme form of control and discipline over African labour. In the early days of the diggings, African workers had built huts for themselves near their work places. Living conditions were squalid and extremely unhealthy, and mine employers found it was very difficult to prevent African workers from deserting when they found their working conditions so unsatisfactory. It was also . . . difficult to prevent the theft and illegal sale of diamonds. . . . As the regime of the individual digger gave way to that of the highly capitalized mining company, so the living conditions of workers were regulated. Eventually, all African labour . . . was housed in closed compounds with no uncontrolled outlet except through a shaft to the mine. Apart from permitting extreme labour discipline and a fuller exploitation of the miners' physical powers, this system of virtual imprisonment made it difficult for the African miners to organize themselves and fight for improved wages and conditions."

other, offering protection to each group while provoking their hatred of each other. When diplomacy failed, the British attacked resistant foes or annexed their territory under threat of attack. Succumbing to this pressure, the Boers surrendered the Transvaal to British control, the Zulu gave up the regions of Natal (which came to be known as British Zululand), and the Ndebele gave up the mineral-rich area which was to become Rhodesia. The British unified much of southern Africa in this way, creating an entirely white-dominated union of Boer, British, and African lands under the constitution of the Union of South Africa in 1910. Now Britain was assured of control of mineral interests.

Both the Act of Union and the growth of the diamond and gold mining industries under the British had significant impacts

Thousands of workers migrated to the Kimberley mine near the De Beers farm when diamonds were discovered there.

on the region of southern Africa. Historian J.D. Omer-Cooper explains the significance of the growth of diamond—and later gold—mining on the economy of the region in his book *History of Southern Africa.*

> The development of the diamond fields began to transform the South African economy. This process was to be carried forward and accelerated by the exploitation of gold at the Witwatersrand. The economy lost its essentially agricultural and pastoral nature and became based on mining and industry. The development of the

diamond fields for the first time made South Africa a fruitful field for large-scale capital investment and opened the way to the establishment of modern industrial capitalism in the country. The new wealth won from the diamond fields and the urgent need for improved communications with the ports led to massive investment in railway building which had been undertaken on only a very limited scale before the diamond discoveries.

The development of the diamond fields and the building of new means of communication intensified economic activity all over South Africa. The white states and the remaining independent African states were drawn into closer association with one another. Expanded markets for agricultural produce were created, providing new opportunities for white commercial farmers but also for African peasants. . . . At the same time . . . expanded economic activity enormously increased demands for African labour.[20]

The roots of the apartheid system also can be seen both in this increased demand for African labor to run white-owned industries and in the formation of the Union of South Africa. When the Union was created, unifying the Orange Free State and the Transvaal with British regions such as Natal and the Cape Colony as well as the former African state of Zululand, the newly formed government included both Boers and British whites, but no black Africans at all. An all-white parliament was set up in Cape Town, and the region was nominally administered by a British governor general and two Boers who were appointed as prime minister and

deputy. English and Afrikaans were given equal status as official languages in the union. African languages, like the African people, were left entirely out of the political process.

Under the effects of the Act of Union, Parliament passed numerous laws limiting the rights of the blacks of South Africa. The Native Land Act banned the buying and selling of land between blacks and whites and relegated blacks to "Native Reserves" on only 13 percent of the region's land. Only blacks employed full time by whites were allowed on white land. And all blacks had to carry passes

Signs like this one were common in South Africa where blacks lived with racist laws and limited rights imposed by an all-white parliament.

showing their employment. A "color bar" was also developed so that blacks could only hold certain kinds of jobs— mostly menial—while top skilled jobs were given to whites. In time these laws were unified under a philosophy and name: apartheid.

Throughout the 1940s until the late 1980s apartheid laws created heartbreaking restrictions on the lives of the black majority of South Africa. Apartheid policy ended when blacks were given the vote in 1994. However, apartheid's legacy would be long lasting on the people of southern Africa.

The Results of European Colonialism

The Europeans who came to southern Africa had one thing in mind: exploiting the region's resources. And in exploiting the region's resources, the Portuguese, Dutch, Germans, and British radically changed the lifestyles, cultures, economies, and political lives of the ethnic groups of southern Africa. By the time each nation of southern Africa had finally gained independence and universal voting rights—in the 1990s—the lifestyles and cultures of many southern African tribes had changed almost beyond recognition.

Chapter 4

Cultural Traditions of Southern African People

Cultural traditions such as the rules people follow in their communities, the rites of passage that ease their journeys through life, and the artistic ways they express themselves ground southern Africans in a rich past. Many cultural traditions have endured for hundreds, if not thousands, of years and have helped southern Africans stay connected with their roots. Some aspects of culture, however, have been profoundly affected and even changed by both historical and modern-day problems and conflicts. Warfare, poverty, and the lingering effects of apartheid have torn at the fragile fabric of culture, challenging old ways and forcing some ethnic groups to develop new rituals to face modern problems. In the face of change, however, southern Africans of every ethnic group have clung to their remaining traditions, looking to traditional rules, roles, and rites of passage to guide them as they face the challenges of the future.

Rules

Every culture uses rules, sometimes codified into law and sometimes unwritten, to help guide its members to act according to traditional cultural values. Rules may be directives, which tell individuals what they must do and why they must do it. Or rules may come in the form of taboos which tell individuals what they must not do under any circumstance. To break a taboo or ignore a directive can have profound consequences to an individual, family, or even an entire ethnic group.

Among the Pedi of South Africa, it is traditionally taboo to cut certain grasses and reeds from the time of planting until the harvest. In studying this taboo, in fact, anthropologist H.O. Monning found it difficult to identify the specific reeds and grasses of the taboo because he was not allowed to cut samples for a botanist to identify.

Due to the taboo . . . only the Pedi names can be given [for the types of grasses]: *Lehlakanoka, Motoolo, Mohlaahla* (all types of reeds or rushes), *Tolwane, Lesehu, Tatasi, Hlaabo, Lebaabi, and Mohlaka* (grasses). These are variously used for thatching, weaving, and making brooms. During the same period, when the crops are on the lands, a woman is also not allowed to *ritela ka pato*, the action of beating a clay floor to flatten and smooth its surface with a wooden instrument. Nor may one drag a branch of a tree, which would raise dust. These actions, or the cutting of the prohibited grasses, result in immediate sanctions against the community as a whole, usually in the form of hail, locusts, or a violent storm which destroys crops. A case was recently brought to court where a number of women had cut *Mohlaahla* rushes many miles away from their home. It was said that hail followed along the route by which they had returned home, destroying all the crops in its way. The three women responsible were then sought out and brought before the court, where they were heavily fined. The seasonal taboos are proclaimed annually by the chief.[21]

Directives are similar to taboos in that there are often believed to be severe consequences for breaking these rules. Among the Ovambo of Botswana, for example, it is traditional to remove, or file down, the two top incisor teeth. The Ovambo believe that if these front teeth are not filed by the time a person dies, and the person dies with clenched teeth, the soul will be unable to escape the body and will remain trapped forever.

Rites of Passage

Rules which deal with life's transitions, like the Ovambo's directive to file the incisors before death, help individuals move through life's stages from birth to death. Rites of passage, ceremonial rituals guiding the passage from one stage to another,

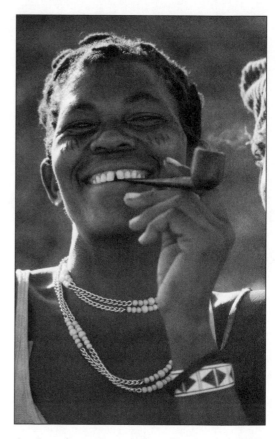

An Ovambo woman smiles, showing her filed-down incisor teeth.

use taboos, directives, and rituals to create bonds between individuals in an ethnic group at each stage of life. Rite of passage ceremonies are conducted at birth, weaning, puberty, marriage, and death. And each ritual helps an individual maintain an intimate connection to his or her ethnic group.

Rites of passage ensure that an individual is connected to his ethnic group from birth. Birth rites take place both at the moment of birth and later, when the new baby and mother are first introduced to the community. Among the San Bushmen of the Kalihari Desert in Botswana, women traditionally give birth alone and conduct certain rituals soon after delivery. Anthropologist Elizabeth Marshall Thomas describes a San Bushmen birth in her book *The Harmless People.*

> When labor starts, the woman does not say what is happening, but lies down quietly on the werf [ground], her face arranged to show nothing, and waits until the pains are very strong . . . though not so strong that she will be unable to walk, and then she goes by herself to the veld, to a place she may have chosen ahead of time and perhaps prepared with a bed of grass. If she has not prepared a place, she gathers what grass she can find and, making a little mound of it, crouches above it so that the baby is born onto something soft. Unless the birth is very arduous and someone else is with the woman, the baby is not helped out or pulled, and when it comes the woman saws its cord off with a stick and wipes it clean with grass. Then the mother collects the stained grass, the placenta, and the bloody sand and covers them all with stones or branches, marking the spot with a tuft of grass stuck up in a bush so that no man will step on or over the place, for the ground where a child has been born is tainted with a power so strong that any man infected with it would lose an aspect of his masculinity, would lose his power to hunt. The woman does not bury the placenta, for if she did she would lose her ability to bear more children.[22]

Among the Xhosa of South Africa, new babies and mothers go through several rituals to ensure their safety and strength in the days following birth. These rituals were described by anthropologist Aubrey Elliott, who lived among the Xhosa. According to Elliott, after a period of confinement during which the child's father may not visit for four days, nor any other men for ten days, the mother and child are welcomed into Xhosa society. In this emergence ritual the mother cleans the hut, smearing the mud walls and floor with fresh cow dung, cleans the baby and herself, and then paints both the baby and herself with paint made of white chalk. She wraps the child in a red blanket, straps it to her back, and allows others to see the baby only if they pay her a small amount of money.

Xhosa Birth Ceremony

Among the Xhosa, birth rites transmit significant cultural values that may be connected with the distrust of outsiders instilled by generations of colonialism and apartheid. According to author Aubrey Elliott in his book *The Magic World of the Xhosa,* the traditional "passing through the smoke" ritual admonishes a child to be faithful to tribe members when faced with probing outsiders.

"The first rite performed on a baby soon after it is born is that of 'passing it through the smoke'. For this, a special fire is made on the mud floor on the wife's side of the hut. . . . When it [the fire] is at its best, the mother cradles the child in her hands and in a rhythmic movement swings it back and forth through the smoke while she chants: 'Deny the things you know. Wush! Wush! Wush! See to it that your mother's ointment pot is never dry. Wush! Wush! Wush!'

This ceremony has tremendous significance in the child's later life because it means he must never betray his friends or give them away. Even though he knows they have done wrong, he is supposed to deny all knowledge and act as if he knew nothing. . . . They are supposed to maintain this stand rigidly until they are given a clearance to divulge the true facts by someone older than or senior to themselves. If, on the other hand, a Xhosa ever does betray a fellow tribesman, then it is because he was 'not passed properly through the smoke when he was born'.

The second phrase in the rite . . . instructs the child not to neglect his mother, but always to give her what she needs. This instruction too is carried out religiously in after years."

These rituals, while having cultural significance as rites of passage, also have practical value. Ritual seclusion may help the baby and mother stay free from illness at their most vulnerable time following birth. And any money paid to the mother for a first peek at the child helps the parents provide for the child in much the same way that an American baby shower gives parents the tools they need to care for their babies.

Initiation and Marriage Rituals

While birth and emergence rituals are essential to giving an individual an initial connection to his ethnic group, a later ritual, that of initiation, solidifies an individual's connection to his or her tribal peers. Initiation is the rite marking the transition from childhood to adulthood. In many southern African ethnic groups today, for both boys and girls, initiation often includes circumcision, the ritual surgical removal or alteration of part of the genitalia.

Among the Sotho of Lesotho, initiation traditionally takes place in initiation schools, where, over a matter of months, groups of boys or girls undergo rituals, learn tribal rules and traditions, and in the end are circumcised. While, due to the influence of Christianity, such schools are less well attended than they once were, some schools still practice these rites of passage. Writer Aubrey Elliott describes his observation of a Sotho circumcision rite:

At sunrise, or thereabouts, the surgeon arrives and can be heard coming in the distance because, as he passes the family huts, the women set up an incessant "Wululululu" wailing which is quite terrifying in effect. . . .

As the doctor comes in sight of the initiates, he starts ranting and abusing and screaming at them and viciously shouts, "Where are these DOGS, where are these THINGS that I have come to make men?" At the same time he loudly exhorts the badness and the evil to be gone out of them so

Xhosa boys perform stick-fighting as part of their initiation into manhood.

The Controversy over Female Circumcision

Throughout Africa, in the initiation rites of many ethnic groups, boys and girls go through an ancient ritual involving circumcision, or the ritual removal or alteration of parts of the genitalia. While male circumcision is not uncommon in the Western world, generally performed on boys when they are babies, female circumcision is quite uncommon outside of Africa and has generated a great deal of controversy on and off that continent.

Advocates of the traditional ritual say that to be fully accepted members of an ethnic group, a girl must undergo the rituals associated with her tribe. They believe circumcision is an essential part of becoming a woman.

Critics of the practice call it "female genital mutilation" and believe that the practice, generally performed in primitive and unsterile conditions by traditional practitioners, is unsafe, cruel, and even deadly. According to the human rights group Amnesty International, an estimated two million girls undergo this surgery every year. Despite its condemnation by the United Nations, and its illegality in many African nations, many southern African ethnic groups continue to defend the practice as an essential cultural tradition.

that they may be men whose childish things are past. The surgeon then suddenly swings his assegai [blade] out drastically in front of the boys and prepares for the operation.

This is done with a deft stroke of the sharpened blade and the boy must not cry out or even flinch in pain.[23]

Girls, too, take part in initiation rituals. Anthropologists William F. Lye and Colin Murray describe a Sotho girls' initiation school.

Girls initiation involves three stages. The first lasts for about a month, during which they are smeared with black clay and do not appear in public. They are enclosed in a special hut in the village. Immediately before they enter this state of seclusion, the mysterious motanyane, the big snake otherwise known as "child of the deep waters", appears to the girls from a deep ravine. . . . The second stage also lasts a month. They are smeared with white clay, and go about in a group performing elaborate songs and dramas which they have learned. A common theme of these is a parody of male behaviour. They also sing mangai, special initiation songs. . . . The third and final stage is the "coming out" when, glistening with red-brown ochre, the girls process slowly through the village. This ritual series transforms girls into marriageable women.[24]

Marriage often marks the end of a girl's initiation period and marks the entry of both men and women into the responsibilities of caring for a family and household. In many southern African ethnic groups, marriages join not only individuals but families and clans, and the union is more than social and spiritual, it is economic. Girls bring valued bridewealth, or marriage gifts, to their fathers' households.

Among the Xhosa of South Africa, in fact, girls are highly valued at birth because of the eventual bridewealth, or *lobolo*, they will bring their fathers when they are married. Bridewealth is the gift of livestock or, today, money, bestowed by a bridegroom on his father-in-law in exchange for the right to marry his daughter. According to Aubrey Elliott,

> The birth of a baby girl in a family creates a great deal of satisfaction because girls bring wealth to their father when, on their marriage, they earn *lobolo* for him from the husband who carries them off. This has given rise to the saying in the tribe that girls are the "cattle of the family". A man with many daughters regards himself as particularly well-favoured.[25]

Wedding rituals in many ethnic groups continue to follow elaborate and expensive traditions, despite the intrusion of Christianity into southern Africa. Even Christian couples will often opt for both Christian and traditional ceremonies tying them to both tribe and church. Writer and artist Barbara Tyrrell interviewed an aging Zulu man, who described his traditional ceremony.

> The day I got married was a great day. The marriage took place at my kraal [homestead], which is the Zulu custom. . . .

A Xhosa bride (right) stands with her attendant in a traditional wedding ceremony in Johannesburg.

A couple combines a modern Christian wedding with Zulu traditions by having a Zulu priest perform part of the ceremony.

The bridal party took up a position in some bush some distance from the kraal where the bride dressed up in all her finery consisting of a leather skirt . . . a long fringe veil made of fibrous leaves . . . and ornamental ropes of twisted calf skin and bead work strung in a coil over her shoulder and under her arm. White cow-tail fringes were bound round both arms and below the knee of each leg. On her right wrist was tied the distended gall-bladder of the goat which was slaughtered for her before she left her father's kraal. . . . She carried a shaftless spear and during the wedding dance ceremony she approached to where I was sitting and presented it to me. This, according to our Zulu customs was the token which clinched the marriage ceremony. With this shaftless spear I pranced about performing, brandishing the spear, extolling my prowess . . . for having achieved a victory in securing Bhekiwe as my first and chief wife.[26]

Honoring the Ancestors

While marriage transforms a young man and woman into a husband and wife, death transforms an individual into an ancestor. For many ethnic groups, death rituals mark both an end of life and a beginning of an afterlife, a way to wield a powerful influence over an ethnic group as an ancestor.

Many ethnic groups require that families undergo elaborate rituals to honor ancestors and help ease the transition from death to ancestry. Among the Tswana, for example, a blanket, made from the skin of an animal slaughtered to honor the dead, must accompany the dead to the afterlife. Authors Colin Murray and William F. Lye describe the ritual.

> A departed spirit for whom no such feast has been held will wander in limbo and return to haunt the living with the complaint, again transmitted in a dream, "Where is my blanket? I am cold." After the period of mourning, a sheep should be slaughtered to remove the pollution which attaches to close kin following a death in the family. In a widow's case . . . cleansing ritual takes place at the widow's natal home. She must be washed with a solution of the sheep's gall in water. Her head is shaved, her nails cut and her mourning clothes burned. Her brother or another close relative must provide her with new clothes. Whatever the circumstances, this ritual should not take place in summer but in winter, after the crops have been reaped, for "what provokes the frost is the mourning clothes."[27]

For the San Bushmen hunter-gatherers of Botswana, death is a time of mourning which marks the true end of life. According to the San folklore, the dead do not rise up again because of an error of a hare, a small rabbitlike animal.

> The moon was the one who ordered the hare to go to tell the people that a man who is ill will rise up, like himself. For he who is the moon, when he dies, he comes again, living.
>
> The hare went, but he turned the story round. He said that a man who dies will not arise; he decreed that a man who dies shall die completely and be finished. That is why people do not rise up. People who die do not arise. Dying, they are finished. Therefore, people who die do not come back living; they die and are completely finished. They do not arise, for they are truly finished. . . .
>
> Therefore we who are ill are finished; we do not rise again. We who are ill, we are finished. Our thoughts, ascending, leave us. Our bodies, our bodies are those which lie in the earth. That is why our thoughts leave us.[28]

The Arts

A culture's thoughts and views of life, death, and basic values are often expressed through the arts: dance, visual arts, music, and games. And each culture's unique view of the world can often be identified in their artwork.

Beadwork has historically played a significant role in cultural identity in southern

San Bushman Litany of Death

The following religious litany on death was written by //Kabbo, a San Bushman of Botswana, and was included in a book called *Stories that Float from Afar: Ancestral Folklore of the San of South Africa*, edited by J.D. Lewis-Williams:

When a Bushman dies,
He goes to this place.

An old man wastes away and dies;
He goes to this place.

An old woman becomes lean;
Her flesh vanishes away;
She dies;
She goes to this place.

A little child who is very small dies;
It too goes to this place.

If a man shoots another with an arrow
And the other dies,
He goes to this place.

If a man cuts another man with a short knife
And the man dies,
He goes to this place.

When a man shoots another with poison,
The man dies from the poison
And goes to this place.

A man stabs another with a dagger;
The other one dies
And goes to this place.

If a man shoots a woman with an arrow
And the woman dies
She goes to this place.

The very old man whose head becomes white,
Dies of hunger;
He goes.

The man who shoots well lives.
The man who shoots amiss dies of hunger.

The very old woman whose flesh is dry,
Dies of hunger.

Abraham is a 110-year-old San Bushman chief. The San Bushmen believe death is the true end of life.

Africa. Many ethnic groups have used beading patterns and personal ornamentation to identify themselves as members of a specific tribe. The Zulu, for example, design elaborate beaded headdresses and hairstyles to be used in ceremonial occasions such as marriages. Traditionally, beadwork signified one's stage of life, as recounted by author Barbara Tyrrell. "At the beginning of courting, a girl will decorate her hair with beads and mealies [powdered grain] and sing as she goes to the waterhole. By these indirect symbols young men will know that she is now on the marriage market."

According to Tyrrell, different colored beads woven into flaps and worn at the neck by young Zulu men are called love letters, and their colors carry different meanings.

A general interpretation is as follows: red, for intense and jealous passion, or eyes red with watching for the beloved; blue for thoughts that fly to the loved one like the wings of doves; yellow, the fullness of gooseberries; white, the long, white road leading to Johannesburg (where many youths go to work in the mines); black, a wish to wear the black leather skirt of marriage; white, also purity and faithfulness; pink or green, poverty, coolness.[29]

Dancing is another form of expressive art which has cultural significance. Many ethnic groups have characteristic dances which are performed for both ceremonial or specific social occasions.

A Zulu woman wears a headdress decorated with elaborate beadwork.

Among Xhosa adolescents, for example, boys and girls will meet for ritual dances in much the same way that American teens meet to dance, talk, and joke. Girls meet together on their days off, carrying sticks and dressed in their best clothes, according to author Aubrey Elliott.

Periodically, they stop to join in light games or fighting with their sticks or just to dance and sing. Their dance is of the same type as that of the boys with emphasis on body movements, the stamping of the feet and on arm movements. They dance individually or in small groups or in large troupes. . . .

In an afternoon's fun the boys mix fighting with dancing. They parade around in large groups and their dance consists of wild jumping and stamping movements to the accompaniment of singing and musical instruments. . . .

Another form of dancing that young Xhosa indulge in is that of a controlled system of vibrating or rippling their chest and abdomen muscles. It is a form of dancing which it seems is practiced almost exclusively by the Xhosa.[30]

Modern Conflicts and Their Effects on Culture

Arts, such as dancing and beadwork, reveal an individual's cultural connections and help strengthen them in the face of challenges such as illness, poverty, and social conflict.

The social conflicts caused by colonialism and the apartheid system tore at the cultural roots of many tribes by forcing them from their traditional lands. The vital connection between people and the land where their ancestors lived and were buried was broken when many tribes were forced to live on nontraditional "reserves." For cultures that rely on their connections to the ancestors for spiritual advice and sustenance, moving away from their homelands meant a certain degree of cultural death.

Forced removals during the apartheid era, in which entire communities were moved to new locations to make room for whites, were not the only reason many southern African ethnic groups lost their cultural connections with the land, however. Poverty has also had the effect of forcing tribes apart as people migrate in search of employment. The migrant labor system, which supplies workers for southern African mining companies, ensures that men are away from their families for much of the year, returning home only occasionally for holidays or special occasions. Under these circumstances, it is difficult to maintain cultural traditions which rely on the steady influence and presence of fathers and young men.

Yet despite the challenges presented by modern society, southern African cultures continue as a dynamic force in the region today. Individuals identify themselves both by their nation: Zimbabwe, Angola, or South Africa, and by tribe: Zulu or Xhosa or Herero. And the young, even on moving away from their roots in the countryside, often continue to return home for traditional ceremonies and rituals, expressing traditional values and beliefs in a modern era.

Chapter 5

Spiritual Traditions of Southern African People

Southern Africa, home to a multitude of ethnic groups speaking dozens of languages, is also home to a great many religious traditions, both indigenous and imported. About two-thirds of southern Africans today are practicing Christians and are members of a variety of denominations. In addition, the majority of southern Africans—including those who identify themselves as Christians—continue to maintain some connection to the religious practices and spiritual beliefs of their ancestors. Because of this underlying current of indigenous African spirituality, some common elements pervade southern African religious life. The practice of religious rituals, the connection to the spirit world, and the reliance on religious leaders for guidance are all common elements of the southern African spiritual experience.

The Spirit World

Many ethnic groups believe in the daily interaction between the human world and the invisible spirit world. Spirits are thought to inhabit people, objects, animals, and places. Even ethnic groups who have adopted Christianity have mixed up their indigenous beliefs about spirits with the Christian belief in a single God. Among the Sotho and Tswana of Lesotho, Botswana, and South Africa, for example, African independent churches incorporate beliefs in ancestral spirits into Christian worship services. Anthropologist Colin Murray cites a 1976 study when he notes that these are Christian churches in which

'ancestral veneration, dance and instrumental ritual are incorporated and validated in Christian terms'. For example, the "holy spirit" (moya), one of the Trinity [the Christian belief in a God in three persons: God the Father, God the Son, and God the Holy Spirit] "grips" people in an idiom very similar to the traditional form of mystical affliction by "spirit of the ancestors".[31]

A Dutch Christian church in South Africa. Christianity has been partially accepted by the native people, who blend its ceremonies with their ancient beliefs.

This mystical affliction, in which a person may shake, sweat, go into convulsions, and "speak in tongues," is traditionally thought to be caused by spirit possession in which a spirit enters the body of a living person.

Ancestral spirits are a major part of the spiritual beliefs of many ethnic groups. Many Africans believe that when people die, they become ancestral spirits who help guide the tribe toward righteousness. According to anthropologist Maija Hiltunen, among the Ovambo of northern Namibia, for example, ancestral spirits hold a great deal of moral authority.

In the minds of people the ancestor spirits no longer have faults. They are continually concerned with proper conduct among their own relatives. Spirits have special moral authority. They may punish moral violations. Ancestral spirits act on their own, but in some cases, they are believed to derive authority from God.

The ancestor spirits must be respected and propitiated [pleased]. If they are personally neglected or their living descendants have disturbed the group's peace, they may cause them sickness or death. The end of this retribution is to maintain group unity and solidarity.[32]

Ancestors are not the only types of spirits believed to influence peoples' lives. The Xhosa of South Africa believe in the "People of the River and the Sea," a race of people that lives under water. According to anthropologist Aubrey Elliott,

To the Xhosa, the "People of the River" exist as surely as does the family next door. They do not doubt that the "People" are there down under the water where their homes are. . . .
The People of the River are kind and good; they protect humans when they go swimming, which explains why a person rises in the water. . . . He is being held up by "them" so that he will not drown. They become worried when earth people swim and so try to discourage them; that is why, on the beach, the waves come rushing up to anyone walking along the sand. . . . 'The People are trying to chase him away from the dangers of the water'.[33]

The Xhosa regularly make offerings to the People to thank them for protections or to ask for their blessings.

The animal, an ox or a goat, is killed in the afternoon inside the cattle kraal of the family making the offering,

and it is skinned where it dies. The carcase is then left on its skin on the spot and when night falls, the family shut themselves in their huts and will

not go outside again, not for anything, until the next morning when it is light. As soon as it gets dark, they say the People of the River come, apparently in spiritual form, and "sit" around the carcase in a circle. They examine it minutely to satisfy themselves that it is really a good offering, and they take minute pieces of the meat which can hardly be noticed the next day . . . then, if they are satisfied with the offering, they thereafter give their everlasting protection to the whole family and join the numbers of spiritual protectors of the homestead called Izilo.[34]

The Izilo are another type of spirit in which the Xhosa believe. They are invisible wild animals in whom the spirits of the ancestors reside, allowing the ancestors to come among their earthly families to watch over them. Other ethnic groups also believe in spirits which reside in wild animals, but these are often visible.

Several ethnic groups believe, for example, that certain animals have magical powers and are used by local witches as assistants or familiars. Among the Ovambo agriculturalists who live in northern Namibia, the owl is thought to assist witches in stealing the souls of sleeping people. And the Xhosa believe that witches ride around at night on baboons and use magical water snakes to cause illnesses in their enemies.

To cure the illnesses and misfortunes caused by encounters with both human and animal spirits, southern Africans turn to a variety of spiritual advisors.

Spiritual Advisors and Leaders

Among nearly every ethnic group, spiritual advisors and leaders perform such services as providing moral and religious guidance, conducting rituals, divining the future and the demands of the spirits, and healing the sick. There are many different types of religious leaders, each with his or her own role to play in the community.

Among the Ovambo, spirit mediums are religious leaders who contact ancestral spirits to discover their wishes, and then advise the living on the best ways to appease angry spirits. Anthropologist Maija Hiltunen describes the role of Ovambo spirit mediums in her book *Witchcraft and Sorcery in Ovambo.*

Goats are sometimes sacrificed as offerings to the Xhosa "People of the River and the Sea" spirits.

Xhosa Witch-Hunts

Many ethnic groups believe in the powers of "witches" to injure ordinary people. When someone becomes ill or has a misfortune, often a witch doctor or diviner is consulted to determine the cause of the problem. And often, the diviner determines that a witch is living in the community and is the source of the misfortune.

Aubrey Elliott, an anthropologist who lived among the Xhosa, recounts a Xhosa witch doctor's methods of discovery in his book *The Magic World of the Xhosa.*

"The witch-doctor sits in a circle formed by the men and women who have engaged him to smell out a witch, or perhaps to find stolen cattle, and he suggests to them why they have come. He is not told in advance why he has been asked to divine, as he has to find this out for himself and then give the audience the answer. For instance, he may start by saying: 'You have come about something with two legs,' and if he is wrong the audience clap and chant: 'We agree.' . . . Then he says: 'No! I am mistaken. It has got four legs.' If he is right the audience say: 'Throw behind,' . . . and their excitement warms up and the diviner gets his clue and goes on, 'It is a cow.' 'No it is an ox.' 'It is black,' or 'it is brown.' The excitement rises in the crowd.

'I can see, it is sick.'

The audience responds: 'Throw behind!'

And so he continues cleverly building up the image in his own mind of what the audience want him to tell them. Then he explains to them that 'the animal is sick because a witch in the neighbourhood sent [spirits] to 'blow medicine over it.' After this, he proceeds to smell out who the witch is and, here again, it is said he always accuses the person whom the audience themselves believe is guilty. Witch-doctors do not always accuse the 'guilty' person outright but hint and, in an indirect manner, leave little doubt who it is. At other times, bolder diviners stand up and point a finger directly in the face of someone in the audience and say, 'There is your witch!'

Such drama always stuns the crowd and they are shocked to find they really have a witch amongst them."

Accused witches are frequently run out of neighborhoods or homesteads, fleeing to live with remote relatives and forced to leave possessions behind.

Spirit mediums who determine the cause of illness or misfortune can be in direct connection with these spirits, which takes place in a state of spirit possession. Important in this context is the medium's moral role.

He is the living spokesman for the spirit's will, the mediator between men and the spirits. The spirit medium exhorts the community to moral conduct. People believe that he has derived his ability from the spirits. When he is under the spirit's influence, he is a sacred and morally authoritative personality; in his everyday life he does not differ from his fellowmen in any way.[35]

Spiritual leaders often have more than simple moral authority: They often are political leaders, as well. Among the Kavango peoples who live along the banks of the Okavango River that runs into Botswana, Namibia, and Angola, local "chiefs" are traditionally spiritual leaders as well as political and economic leaders. Often, these leaders gained political strength because they had powers considered magical in their communities. According to anthropologist Thomas J. Larson, among the Mbukushu, a tribe of Kavango people living in Botswana, religious and political leaders traditionally gained much of their power as rainmakers.

> Formerly, the Mbukushu came under one paramount chief, the fumu or fumushokura ("elder chief"), the spiritual leader and the great rainmaker. . . . A chief would not tolerate one of his subjects possessing more cattle or any other form of wealth than himself. He could have such a person accused of sorcery and put to death. On the other hand, a chief was responsible for making rain, and thus providing good harvests, and for assuring the general welfare of his people.[36]

Rainmaking was an important leadership skill among people living in the dry, dusty edges of the Kalihari Desert. Today, as in the past, spiritual leaders such as rainmakers use a variety of spiritual objects and methods such as divination to determine when the rains will come. Divination, or contact with the spirit world, can involve the use of magical objects or herbs. Diviners often throw special stones or shells and "read" the positions in which they fall, or "read" the entrails of a sacrificed animal. According to anthropologist Colin Murray, the Sotho and Tswana people have several methods of divination. "There are various methods of divination, of which the most common is the use of a set of divining objects (ditaola) whose 'falls' the specialist interprets. Whatever the technique, effective divination requires communion with the ancestors. Some doctors use snuff to 'clear the wits', the more easily to achieve this communion."[37]

Herbs such as snuff are also used by two other types of traditional spiritual leaders: herbalists and "witch doctors." Among the Xhosa, herbalists use plants, rituals, and traditional medicines to immunize and protect vulnerable people. Aubrey Elliot writes, "A herbalist's training, unlike that of a witch-doctor, which consists of spiritual tuition, is physical. He is taught the use of herbs and how to make other medicines by his father . . . or he can be taught by another herbalist over a number of years."[38] Witch doctors, on the other hand, are diviners who use similar tools and methods as the herbalists to cure illnesses and heal people who have been bewitched.

Female witch doctors in traditional dress tell fortunes by divining bones that have been thrown down.

Spiritual Objects and Places

The plants used by herbalists and the objects used by diviners are some of the things found in nature that are thought to have spiritual powers. Among many ethnic groups, many natural places also are thought to have religious significance. Among the Herero of Namibia, for example, a special Omumborumbonga tree was traditionally thought to be the original point of descent for the first Herero ancestors who emerged from heaven to settle on the earth, and was thus considered to be sacred.

Among the Xhosa of South Africa, a special coastal rock called Cove Rock, near East London, South Africa, is thought to contain the entry point to the underwater kingdom of the People of the Sea, and thus be imbued with spiritual power. According to anthropologist Aubrey Elliott,

> The Xhosa in those parts say that the channel between the two rocks is the gateway to the home of the underwater people. At night when the tide is high and the sea floods through it far up on to the beach, they believe that the People come with it to play in the shallow water on the sand. . . .

In the sea, at the back of the main section of Cove Rock, the water has hewn large caverns into the stone and the sea comes pounding into them to send clouds of spray high up into the air. The local Xhosa say these caverns are the doorways to the homes of the underwater folk. They say it is quite clear that the whole rock is hollow underneath because of the sound the water makes as it hits it. They think that the place below where "they" sleep is quite dry, even though there is plenty of water all around.[39]

Spiritual places and natural objects are often used in rituals to contact and appease the spirit world. And religious rituals are an essential aspect of southern African religious life.

Rituals, Festivals, and Celebrations

Religious rituals, festivals, and celebrations are held in every community of southern Africa, allowing practitioners to act together in connecting with divine or creative spirits, gods, or God. Some rituals are held to ask for intervention in the difficulties of life, others are held to ask for-

The Xhosa and the People of the Sea

The Xhosa people have many stories about the People of the Sea, some ancient, and others based on recent experiences. Sometimes these stories are meant to explain natural phenomenon, fortune, and misfortune. The following story was recorded by Aubrey Elliott in his book *The Magic World of the Xhosa*.

"Once, many years ago, Lolombela says, one of them [the People of the Sea] was left by the tide and could not get back to the water because 'they cannot walk far on dry land.' The next day a Xhosa man found him. The creature cried bitterly. He was full of sand and his usually-shiny skin was stiff and parched. In his language he begged and cried to be taken back to the water but the man could not understand him and, instead of doing so, carried him off to the farmer's home. . . . 'But,' Lolombela said, 'If only that Xhosa had used his brains and taken the creature back to the water, his fortune would have been made because the underwater people repay kindness with great and rich gifts.' He says they have different ways of returning kindness and, among others, they let the water wash a present up at a person's feet as he walks along the beach or beside the river. 'It looks just as if it happened by accident, but it is not an accident.'"

A group of men dance as part of a religious celebration. Rituals, festivals, and celebrations are held to honor the gods and spirits.

giveness or atone for misdeeds. Celebrations and festivals allow religious communities to give thanks for the good things they have received in life. These religious rituals, celebrations, and festivals can include prayer, sacrifices, drama, dancing, and music.

Ethnic groups conduct a variety of rituals to give thanks for the good things they have received in life. While African Christian churches may decorate their altars with the bounty of the harvest, those practicing indigenous African religions may sacrifice an animal to show their gratitude.

Among the Zulu, the largest ethnic group in South Africa, anthropologist Harriet Ngubane reports that "The ancestors are thanked from time to time by a sacrifice known as ukubonga, thanksgiving." She says, "A goat or an ox [is sacrificed] to thank the ancestors for good things of life, e.g. a good win at the races, or a good job, or a generally satisfactory life."[40]

Thanksgiving is not the only reason ethnic groups such as the Zulu conduct rituals in which animals are sacrificed. Ngubane recounts that animals also can be sacrificed as a way of asking the ancestors or other spirits for assistance with difficult tasks or problems. "A goat [is sacrificed] to ask for the blessing of the ancestors before undertaking any major or risky task, e.g. before going out to major cities to seek employment." Or, "A goat [is sacrificed] to appease the ancestors if there is evidence that they had been annoyed."[41]

The San Bushmen, hunter-gatherers of Botswana, also ask assistance in difficult tasks such as hunting, but traditionally they may pray to the new moon rather than their ancestors. According to San folklore recorded by J.D. Lewis-Williams in *Stories that Float from Afar*,

"They cannot ask the sun for anything, but they do ask the moon. They raise the right hand and say, 'I speak with the hand here, so that I may kill a springbok with my hand, with my bow.'

'I lie down. I ask that I may kill a springbok early tomorrow. . . .'

The moon lies there in the sky. . . . After the moon has died and come out again small, the /Xam-ka!ei speak to it."[42]

God and Gods

While many groups appeal to the spirits of their ancestors for assistance in life's difficulties, some ethnic groups pray to God or gods. Different groups conceive of a creative and intervening force, or God, in different ways. The Dobe !Kung, an ethnic group related to the San Bushmen and living in the Kalihari Desert at the border of Namibia and Botswana, have several, often conflicting, beliefs, says anthropologists Richard B. Lee.

The !Kung have two major deities, a high god called //gangwan!an!a (big, big god) and by other names, who is sometimes connected with the elephant Kau in the myths, and //gangwa matse (small //gangwa), the trickster god. . . .

There are varying opinions about the nature of these two deities. In some myths, the high god is portrayed as good and the lesser god as evil. In others the roles are reversed. Some !Kung regard big //gangwa as a creator, remote and inaccessible, and see small //Gangwa as the destroyer, the main source of death. Other !Kung insist that it is the high god who is both the creator and the killer.[43]

The Zulu people traditionally believed in many different gods, and while today most practice Christianity, vestiges of the old beliefs remain. Anthropologist Barbara Tyrrell describes one of the traditional Zulu gods in her book *Tribal Peoples of Southern Africa*.

There is a vague spirit named Nomkubulwana, a female who may be glimpsed in the mists of the marshes. She is the spirit of ease and plenty, and when there is drought, with accompanying loss of cattle and crops, a special mealie [grain] land must be planted for her. Also a girl must be

The Now of the San Bushmen

The San Bushmen of the Kalihari Desert of Botswana and Namibia believe in a supernatural essence that inhabits an individual from birth. Akin to the Judeo-Christian concept of the soul, this essence called the *Now* connects a person to the spirits and energies of the natural world. Anthropolosist Elizabeth Marshall Thomas describes the *Now* in her book *The Harmless People*.

"The moment of birth is a very important one for the child and for the mother; it is at this moment that the child acquires a power, or an essence, over which he has no control, although he can make use of it. It will last him all his life; it is a supernatural essence that forever after connects the person born with certain forces in the world around him: with weather, with childbearing, with the great game antelope, and with death, and this essence is called the *now*.

There are two kinds of *now*, a rainy or cold one, and a hot and dry one. If a person has a wet *now* and burns his hair in a fire or urinates in a fire, the person's *now* is said to make the weather turn cold (if it is the dry season) or to bring rain (if it is the rainy season). If a person has a dry *now* and burns hair or urinates in a fire, the *now* is said to stop a cold spell or a bad storm. When a person dies, too, the weather changes violently according to the person's *now*. After a death, scorching droughts or devastating storms are sure to follow. . . .

Now is intangible, mystic, and diffuse, and the Bushmen themselves do not fully understand its workings. They do not know how or why *now* changes weather but only that it does."

A Bushman woman stands with her two children. At the moment of birth, a baby acquires its Now, *or essence.*

buried to her neck to appease her. In addition to these observances, girls must borrow the dress of their brothers and take over the male duties of herding, thus to shame Nomkubulwana into bringing rain.[44]

Many ethnic groups believe in a supreme God as well as lesser gods, and this seems to correspond well with the Christian and Muslim beliefs, making conversions to world religions easier and the boundaries between religions vague. According to anthropologists William F. Lye and Colin Murray, "Most Sotho-Tswana today are nominally Christians. Most also continue to revere their ancestors. Having grown up in an environment where Christian and indigenous sources of belief have been integrated for so long, people seldom bother to interpret the two theological traditions independently."[45] Lye and Murray's study of Sotho-Tswana religious activity and belief also found "a widespread uniformity of belief, albeit eclectic and inconsistent, underlying an institutional diversity of religious affiliation. In other words, people believe much the same, but they belong to many different churches."[46]

This observation about the Sotho-Tswana is true for many ethnic groups in southern Africa. While world religions such as Christianity and, to a lesser extent, Islam, have claimed a multitude of converts throughout the region, indigenous African beliefs and rituals continue to influence the day-to-day lives of the people of southern Africa.

Chapter 6

Southern Africa Today—Problems and Promises

Southern Africa today is a region of tremendous hope and promise. In recent years, southern Africa has seen the end of apartheid and the creation of a voting black populace in South Africa, the growth of free and independent nations throughout the region, and the end of a decades-long conflict in Angola. But such gains do not mean that southern Africa is now a region without problems. The legacies of apartheid, colonialism, and Cold War politics have scarred the region deeply. The intertwined problems of political and social instability, poverty, and poor health continue to plague a populace longing for peace and prosperity.

Poverty and Economic Underdevelopment

Poverty continues to plague the majority of southern African people despite the tremendous resources of the region as a whole. One reason for this continuing poverty is the export of resources to foreign nations resulting from years of colonial rule and apartheid.

Colonial rule influenced the modern-day economies of southern African nations by creating systems for extracting the African wealth for the benefit of the colonial nations and investing little in the development of the region. This colonial-type extraction continues today as southern Africa's wealth is exported for the benefit of large corporations and to repay foreign loans. According to political analyst Colin Legum, "Every year, still more capital continues to flow out of Africa to Western Europe, the United States, and Japan than comes into the continent. The outflow is accounted for by interest and redemption of foreign debt and profits from oil and mining ventures."[47]

The mining industry in South Africa, Zimbabwe, Namibia, and Botswana provides migrant-labor jobs to many southern African families, but continues to send much of its profits abroad while providing only low wages for hard labor. And because laborers must migrate for work, mining jobs are also a potential source of

A man stands in front of his shack in Soweto, South Africa. Poverty continues to plague underdeveloped areas of southern Africa.

economic and social instability. According to a study of mine laborers from Lesotho by C. Murray, quoted by author Morag Bell in *Contemporary Africa: Development, Culture and the State*, migrant mine labor has created a culture of dependency in which nearly 70 percent of rural household incomes are derived from migrant labor. Bell's book says that "With the growing trend towards the 'internalization' and 'stabilization' of the workforce within South Africa, the insecurity of their future careers as mine workers is becoming increasingly apparent."[48]

The stability of rural communities in Lesotho, Mozambique, and other areas of southern Africa may be threatened if South Africa chooses to use only South African laborers to work in its mines. If mines are closed to foreign workers, as has happened periodically, millions of people would be thrown into abject poverty. If rural communities are to bring themselves out of poverty, they must have sources of income other than migrant mine work.

Mines are not the only commercial venture drawing workers away from home. Commercial farms, producing crops for export, also attract migrant workers and also are the source of many economic ills. These mostly white-owned farms have been hiring low-wage migrant workers since colonial times, when whites took over traditional tribal lands, forcing Africans to migrate to lands with poorer soil and water resources. Unable to make a living in their new homes, Africans began migrating back to their former lands as farm workers, seeking wages to work on the land they once owned. Today, in Namibia, Zimbabwe, and South Africa, large-scale farms continue to thrive, encouraged by government policies which focus on agriculture for export rather than Africa's traditional economic base: small-scale agriculture for subsistence.

This focus on cash crops has been problematic since colonial times. According to historian Basil Davidson, growing cash crops to the exclusion of food crops has been disastrous for African economies.

Another reason why it was desirable to cut down on cash crops grown for export was the need to produce more food. Wherever cash crop production became important in an African country, shortages of local food began to be felt. This was partly because the more land and labour that was taken for growing cash crops, the less land and labour was there left for growing food. Local food shortages began to be acute, in some countries, as early as the Second World War. Even local famine broke

out in the worst cases: as for example, in northern Mozambique where the Portuguese forced farmers to grow cotton instead of food. Cotton, these farmers rightly said, became "the mother of poverty."[49]

Despite the incidence of rural agricultural poverty in southern Africa, however, hope abounds. In South Africa, the majority of citizens, even those living in urban areas, currently have access to some rural lands for farming or grazing animals. In addition, new policies of land reparations in South Africa offer hope to thousands of landless citizens. Land reparations return land to its original owner or others in need.

In South Africa, the postapartheid government is taking an organized approach to land reparations. The government is slowly buying up the land of willing farmers and redistributing it in a formal and legal manner to families in need, as well as providing them with educational assistance to ensure that they will be able to produce enough food to support their families. New land grants give hope and independence to ethnic groups who were once forced to migrate to cities, mines, and white-owned farms for work.

Economic hope also lies in the political changes of the 1990s. The end of apartheid and the increased political stability of the region has allowed much of southern Africa to unite in an economic trading bloc, the South African Customs Union, a union which was impossible under the white-led apartheid regime. This trading

Cash crops such as cotton have been a source of poverty rather than prosperity as they lead to shortages of food crops and even famine.

union has the potential to open borders, freeing regional trade and allowing prosperity to flow from the richer areas of the region to those enmeshed in poverty.

Political Instability

Poverty is only one of many reasons southern Africa has seen a great deal of political and social instability in the past decade. Another lingering cause of political instability is the so-called Cold War between capitalist countries and Communist countries that ended with the fall

of the Soviet Union in the late 1980s. As part of the Cold War in the 1950s through the 1980s, the United States, South Africa, the Soviet Union, and Cuba funded and encouraged wars in Angola, Mozambique, and Namibia. And in many ways, the social, political, and economic lives of these nations are still in recovery.

In Angola, the civil war that began and grew with Cold War support has only recently seen signs of resolution. This is largely due to the death of one man, rebel leader Jonas Savimbi, who was killed by government forces in February 2002. On April 5, 2002, the *Los Angeles Times* newspaper reported that after more than twenty-five years of civil war, the Angolan government and the rebel group known as the National Union for the Total Independence of Angola, or UNITA, had finally signed a cease-fire agreement.

The cease-fire paves the way for the first period of peace Angolans have known

Land Reparations and Violence over Ownership of Farms in Zimbabwe

In Zimbabwe, land reparations are taking place through violent means. Wealthy white farmers, who have lived on and developed their land for generations, have been forced off their farms by bands of armed squatters. When the landowner is scared off, the land is often divided up among these squatters, though these new farmers are given little education on effective farming techniques.

The squatters are often political supporters of Robert Mugabe, who was re-elected president of Zimbabwe in 2002 in what most foreign observers believe to have been a fraudulent election. The land redistribution is seen by many as payment for political support in the elections. According to an article in the Zimbabwean newspaper, *The Independent*, in March 2002, farm violence has grown in recent years.

"Zimbabwe's commercial farming sector was this week gripped by fear as a terror campaign to force farmers off their land was stepped up following President Mugabe's re-election.

In what is seen as a direct response to his call to intensify farm seizures a white commercial farmer, Terrence Ford of Gowrie Farm in Norton, was bludgeoned to death on Monday by suspected Zanu PF supporters and war veterans [Mugabe supporters].

The suspects had been living on his property since farm invasions began in 2000. . . .

Commercial Farmers Union president Colin Cloete has confirmed an increase in incidents of violence on the commercial farms countrywide.

'Incidents of harassment, trashing and looting, forced evictions and extortion as well as political retribution have reached alarming proportions,' he said yesterday.

'A large proportion of the incidents seem to be retribution against farmers who were exercising their democratic right to support the political party of their choice.' . . .

The mayhem on the farms will perpetuate the food shortages affecting the country as hundreds of farms have now been abandoned in the wake of the violence."

The death of Jonas Savimbi, leader of the National Union for the Total Independence of Angola, in 2002 led to a cease-fire in Angola's civil war.

jority, took up arms against government troops belonging to the Popular Movement for the Liberation of Angola, or MPLA.

The conflict between UNITA and MPLA became a Cold War affair. The United States and South Africa's then-apartheid government supported UNITA against the Marxist MPLA government, which received weapons and fighters from Cuba and the Soviet Union.

The civil war devastated Angolans. About 1.5 million people, according to CIA estimates, have been killed in the conflict. An additional 4.5 million of the country's 13 million people were driven into refugee camps and temporary shelters far from their home villages.[50]

Even after the Cold War ended and Angola's president was elected in what was widely regarded as free and fair elections, Savimbi continued to wage civil war against the government, refusing to accept that the country had moved on to a new era and that he was not in charge.

Savimbi's death heralds a new era for Angola. Joao Porto, an Angolan specialist with the Institute for Security Studies, quoted in the *Los Angeles Times*, sums up the nation's hopes for the future. "'This is what each Angolan has been waiting for for decades, a chance to develop the country in peace and normalcy.'"[51]

since 1960. According to the *Los Angeles Times* report,

Angolans, who fought a 14-year armed struggle against Portuguese rule, have known little but conflict since they gained independence in 1975. That was when Savimbi, who saw himself as the champion of the country's disenfranchised black ma-

The Long-Term Effects of Apartheid

The end of apartheid, as well, has created an opportunity for South Africa's people to develop their nation in peace and normalcy. But this is not to say that the effects of apartheid are no longer apparent. The legacy of apartheid can still be felt throughout the region. Socially and politically, the effects of years of living under

The Angolan Civil War and the Diamond Trade

Diamonds were used to fund the quarter-century-long civil war in Angola since the 1980s. Because of this misuse of the nation's vast resources, 75 percent of Angolan citizens live in poverty. According to the *Los Angeles Times* newspaper,

"Angola, about twice the size of Texas, is one of Africa's richest countries, with vast oil, diamond and fishing reserves. Little of that wealth trickles down to ordinary people. . . .

For a quarter of a century, the warring parties funded the conflict by selling oil and diamonds. UNITA [Savimbi's rebel group] sold diamonds from several mines it controlled and bought weapons with the proceeds."

UNITA procured diamonds in a number of ways and then, according to Fred Bridgland, author of *Jonas Savimbi: A Key to Africa*, a biography of the rebel leader, they were sold on the black market worldwide.

"The diamonds were stolen during raids on MPLS [government political unit] diamond mining centres; smuggled out of mines by underground members of UNITA; and sieved from workings known to UNITA from old Portuguese mineralogical maps. In 1986, UNITA's mining team bought three frogmen's suits in Europe so that diamonds could be recovered from gravel at the bottom of Lunda Province's deeper rivers. Oxygen tanks moved up regularly to Lunda on the backs of porters."

Later, the diamonds were taken by UNITA operatives to Geneva, Switzerland, where they were sold to clients from India, New York, Belgium, and Israel. By the late 1980s, the diamond trade was netting UNITA between $50 thousand and $4 million a month, all of it going to maintain the civil war and none of it used to improve the lives of ordinary Angolans.

A worldwide boycott of Angolan diamonds was enacted in the 1990s to try to stem the flow of this ill-gotten trade. But because it is difficult to identify the true source of a diamond, many Angolan diamonds reached the market and were sold to unsuspecting consumers in jewelry stores all over the world.

apartheid helped create a nationwide culture of noncompliance and distrust of authority in South Africa. Perhaps as a result of apartheid era politics, South Africa has one of the highest crime rates in the world and a very active black-market economy.

Apartheid did more damage than simply creating a distrust of authority, however. It also exacerbated tribalism, the identification with a tribe or ethnic group and the distrust of other ethnic groups. South Africa and other parts of southern Africa such as Zimbabwe and Lesotho continue to face instability caused by tribalism.

In South Africa, for example, political divisions on tribal lines between the African National Congress, or ANC, and the largely Zulu Inkatha Freedom Party resulted in widespread violence for many years. And in Lesotho, tribalism led to widespread rioting when the Lesotho Defence Forces, members of one tribe, were pitted against the nation's leaders as nationwide election results were disputed in 1998.

Rioting and ethnic violence have also been problems in Zimbabwe, often as a result of political divisions. In recent years squatters, people living on land illegally, have taken over the nation's white-owned farms, killing farmers and ruining crops, resulting in widespread food shortages. These squatters, political supporters of President Robert Mugabe, are believed to have gained their land in exchange for support during what is widely regarded as a fraudulent and corrupt presidential election.

Corruption and violence are not unique to Zimbabwe. Official corruption has plagued Namibia and South Africa as well. In South Africa, nepotism, the hiring of relatives in official positions, has been a major issue confronting the ruling party, the ANC. And in Namibia, the president tried to hang onto power by altering the constitution to allow him to remain in power beyond his term.

Hopes for Peace and Stability

But not every nation of the region struggles with corruption. Botswana and Swaziland both have been models of peace and stability since achieving independence. And in South Africa, hope could be seen in the 1999 anticorruption summit which looked at proposals to curb official corruption by removing corrupt officials from office.

In South Africa, efforts also have been made to bring an end to the political divisions, hatred, and violence caused by decades of apartheid through a process known as the Truth and Reconciliation Commission. Hearings held by the Commission in the late 1990s offered tremendous promise in reconciling the differences of South Africans following the pain of the apartheid era. These hearings, led by respected Bishop Desmond Tutu, offered South Africans of every race an opportunity to bring forward crimes and injustices committed during the apartheid era for public hearing and reconciliation. Victims and perpetrators of crimes confronted one another, airing their

Bishop Desmond Tutu led hearings aimed at reconciling the deep divisions caused by decades of apartheid.

differences and, in many cases, arriving at truth, forgiveness, and peace after years of pain.

Health Care: A Problem for the New Millennium

While the political and economic arenas have seen tremendous progress in southern Africa in recent years, the physical pain and health care crises plaguing the people of the region have changed little. Overpopulation due to high birthrates, high infant mortality, malnutrition, and the high incidence of debilitating diseases are among many health problems facing southern Africans today.

High birthrates and the resulting increase in population are a health problem as well as an economic and environmental problem, according to political analysts April A. Gordon and Donald L. Gordon's book *Understanding Contemporary Africa.* Citing a World Bank report, the Gordons write,

Unless rapid population growth is checked, increasing demands for such necessities as food, services, land, and jobs will overwhelm the fragile economies of all but a few African countries. . . . It is also pointed out that while enormous areas of Africa are sparsely populated and underdeveloped, much of this land is unsuitable for intensive human use without costly investment. And given the current population pressure on land and resources in Africa, severe or even irreversible ecological damage is already undermining the environment upon which Africa's development and future populations will depend. . . . The pressures of population, it is claimed, threaten to reverse Africa's development efforts. Population control measures must be implemented if development is to take place.[52]

Family planning programs in southern Africa have been somewhat successful in slowing the birthrate in the region. According to the Gordons,

Although the process of fertility decline is likely to remain gradual and uneven, there is evidence that sub-Saharan Africa is beginning to embark on the road to "demographic transition" from high to low fertility. The increase in contraceptive usage and somewhat smaller family size among younger women are two such signs. Surveys in many countries show a greater interest in family planning and a reconsideration of the benefits of a large family.[53]

The Devastating Spread of HIV/AIDS

Family planning campaigns, particularly those emphasizing the use of condoms, have also been helpful in curbing the spread of AIDS in southern Africa. AIDS, or acquired immunodeficiency syndrome, is caused by the human immunodeficiency virus, or HIV, and is spread through the exchange of body fluids, usually during sexual contact or intravenous drug use. HIV/AIDS is arguably the worst of many health care crises to hit the region this cen-

Mothers and their children visit a clinic specially designed to treat women with HIV/AIDS.

tury, and has the potential of not only devastating the populations of South Africa, Zimbabwe, Botswana, and other nations of the region, but of swamping their economies as well.

In some southern African nations HIV infects as much as 22 percent of the adult population, and that percentage is expected to continue to rise. Because it most often affects young adults in their prime years as economic producers and workers, AIDS is affecting the economy of the region dramatically by both debilitating and killing workers. The annual study, *South Africa Survey 1999/2000*, reports that

> The population growth rate was projected to fall significantly by 2010 as a result of AIDS. It was estimated that by 2010 the population growth rate would drop by 71 percent owing to AIDS. It was also estimated that some six million people in South Africa would be HIV positive by 2005, with more than 18 percent of the workforce infected by 2005.[54]

Children at a hospital with a special program for orphans with AIDS sit around a table for a meal. Thousands of southern African children are infected with HIV.

The largest percentage of those infected today are women. HIV infects women in southern Africa more than men, probably in part due to the inability of a woman in many southern African cultures to deny sexual relations with her husband or de-

mand that he use a condom, even if he is infected with HIV himself. In parts of Botswana and South Africa, over 30 percent of women test positive for HIV in tests given after birth. And because HIV is easily transferred from mothers to babies, in the womb or through breast-feeding, thousands of children have been infected as well. In fact, because of AIDS, the child mortality, or death, rate in Zimbabwe has nearly tripled from 40 to 115.2 out of every 1,000 children.

Children are often affected by the AIDS epidemic even if they do not have the disease themselves. In 1999 Dr. Manto Tshabalala-Msimang, South African minister of health, estimated that by 2005, one million children would be orphaned as a

Saving Children from Pollution-Borne Killers

Diseases caused by pollution in the air and water kill thousands of children worldwide every day. Often these environmental illnesses cause diarrhea, which is easily treated in developed nations. In southern Africa, however, diarrhea often leads to death. According to a 2002 study by the United Nations entitled "Pollution-Related Diseases Kill Millions of Children A Year," quoted on the website of the World Health Organization,

"Almost one-third of the global disease burden can be attributed to environmental risk factors. Over 40 percent of this burden falls on children under five years of age, who account for only 10 percent of the world's population. A major contributing factor to these diseases is malnutrition which affects around 150 million and undermines their immune systems. Malnutrition and diarrhoea form a vicious cycle. The organisms that cause diarrhoea harm the walls of a children's guts, which prevents them digesting and absorbing their food adequately, causing even

greater malnutrition—and vulnerability to disease."

The United Nations as well as the governments of southern Africa are taking steps to ensure that the children of the region have access to clean water and health care. Another important step in preventing deaths from diarrhea is increasing children's access to oral rehydration formulas.

Oral rehydration formulas are medical packets containing salts and sugars which can be added to clean water to help the body regain its fluids. Because diarrhea often causes death through dehydration—children lose so much water so quickly that they literally die of thirst—the most important step in saving a child is rehydration. Oral rehydration formulas can be given by a child's family—no special medical personnel needs to be involved. By increasing public access to these important health care tools, the United Nations hopes to save the lives of thousands of children each year.

Young girls carry buckets of water from one of eight wells that supply a shantytown of 350 squatters.

result of AIDS. And in Zimbabwe, a 1995 report in the *Charlotte Observer* newspaper estimated that by 2010 one-third of all children would be orphaned. And even if they do not lose their parents, the presence of AIDS in their community increases the incidence of other diseases to which children are often susceptible, such as tuberculosis, or TB, a deadly disease of the lungs.

The epidemic of TB in southern Africa is closely related to the incidence of AIDS. Because people with HIV and AIDS have suppressed immune systems and are unable to fight off illness, they often catch diseases like TB more easily. Because TB is caused by airborne bacteria, children— even those without HIV/AIDS—are sus-

ceptible to catching it from infected persons with whom they have close contact, such as teachers and parents.

The epidemic of TB highlights an important fact about southern African health care. TB is a highly treatable disease and often can be cured with regular doses of antibiotics. However, because many people lack access to doctors, hospitals, and medicines, many with TB go inadequately treated or completely untreated, allowing the disease to spread farther and more quickly than it would if better access to health care were available.

Access to health care, clean water, and good nutrition are some of the greatest health care problems facing southern Africa today. Each year millions of children in Africa die of diseases which have been virtually wiped out in the developed world or of malnutrition due to poor access to adequate food. But hope lies in the concerted efforts of national governments and the United Nations to solve these problems.

The United Nations fund for children, UNICEF, is currently campaigning to bring better access to health care to children throughout Africa. The campaign includes immunizations against common diseases, as well as medicines and preventative measures to help eradicate diseases such as malaria, for which there are no immunizations available. In addition, the South African government has made a concerted effort to immunize more children against such childhood illnesses as measles and to increase public access to clean water and adequate nutrition.

Public health campaigns have also slowed the spread of AIDS, though not as much as is needed, according to April A. Gordon and Donald L. Gordon, editors of *Understanding Contemporary Africa.*

Public health campaigns to educate the public, distribute or encourage the use of condoms, safeguard blood supplies, and discourage risky sexual activity have been launched across the continent. In fact, Africa is considered to be in many ways a pioneer in AIDS prevention as a result of its creative radio and TV campaigns and efforts to promote safe sex and condom use. . . .

While such efforts are vital in the war against AIDS, they are unlikely to stop the relentless advance of the disease for some time to come.[55]

While southern African nations have had many successes economically and politically, the greatest challenges to the nations today may be in insuring the health and safety of their most important asset: their human resources.

Notes

Introduction: Southern Africa, Land of Extremes

1. Jocelyn Murray, ed., *Cultural Atlas of Africa*. Oxford, England: Phaidon Press, 1981, p. 24.
2. Murray, *Cultural Atlas of Africa*, p. 24.

Chapter 1: Lifestyles of Southern African People

3. *Los Angeles Times*, "Lesotho: Educating Young Herders," June 9, 2002, p. A13.
4. Murray, *Cultural Atlas of Africa*, p. 80.
5. Gordon D. Gibson, Thomas J. Larson, and Cecilia R. McGurk, *The Kavango Peoples*. Wiesbaden, Germany: Franz Steiner, 1981, pp. 106–107.
6. Jiro Tanaka, *The San: Hunter-Gatherers of the Kalahari*. Tokyo: University of Tokyo Press, 1980, p. 10.

Chapter 2: Indigenous Kingdoms of Southern Africa

7. Kevin Shillington, *History of Africa*. New York: St. Martin's Press, 1995, p. 139.
8. Martin Hall, *The Changing Past: Farmers, Kings and Traders in Southern Africa*, 200–1860. Cape Town: David Philip, 1987, pp. 67–72.
9. D.T. Niane, ed., *Africa from the Twelfth to the Sixteenth Century*, Vol. 4 of UNESCO *General History of Africa*. London: Heinemann and the University of California Press, 1984, p. 594.
10. Hall, *The Changing Past*, p. 64.
11. Kevin Shillington, *A History of Southern Africa*, Essex, England: Longman Group, 1987, p. 15.
12. Shillington, *History of Africa*, p. 145.
13. Niane, *Africa from the Twelfth to the Sixteenth Century*, p. 547.
14. Hall, *The Changing Past*, pp. 96–97.
15. Shillington, *History of Africa*, p. 144.
16. Shillington, *A History of Southern Africa*, p. 44.

Chapter 3: Europeans in Southern Africa

17. Shillington, *History of Africa*, p. 201.
18. B.A. Ogot, ed., *Africa from the Sixteenth to the Eighteenth Century*, Vol. 5 of UNESCO *General History of Africa*. London: Heinemann and the University of California Press, 1992, p. 631.
19. J.F. Ade Ajayi, *Africa in the Nineteenth Century Until the 1880s*, Vol. 6 of UNESCO *General History of Africa*. London: Heinemann and the University of California Press, 1989, pp. 161–62.

20. J.D. Omer-Cooper, *History of Southern Africa.* Portsmouth, NH: Heinemann Educational Books, 1987, pp. 101–103.

Chapter 4: Cultural Traditions of Southern African People

21. H.O. Monning, *The Pedi.* Pretoria, South Africa: J.L. Van Schaik, 1967, p. 69.

22. Elizabeth Marshall Thomas, *The Harmless People.* New York: Vintage Books, 1989, p. 157.

23. Aubrey Elliott, *The Magic World of the Xhosa.* London: William Collins Sons & Co., 1970, p. 84.

24. William F. Lye and Colin Murray, *Transformations on the Highveld: The Tswana and Southern Sotho.* Totowa, NJ: Barnes and Noble, 1980, p. 125.

25. Elliott, *The Magic World of the Xhosa,* p. 62.

26. Barbara Tyrrell, *Tribal Peoples of Southern Africa.* Cape Town: Books of Africa, 1968, p. 120.

27. Lye and Murray, *Transformations on the Highveld,* p. 126.

28. J.D. Lewis-Williams, ed., *Stories that Float from Afar: Ancestral Folklore of the San of South Africa.* College Station: Texas A&M University Press, 2000, p. 253.

29. Tyrrell, *Tribal Peoples of Southern Africa,* p. 116.

30. Elliott, *The Magic World of the Xhosa,* pp. 70–71.

Chapter 5: Spiritual Traditions of Southern African People

31. Lye and Murray, *Transformations on the Highveld,* p. 132.

32. Maija Hiltunen, *Witchcraft and Sorcery in Ovambo,* Helsinki: The Finnish Anthropological Society, 1986, pp. 56–57.

33. Elliott, *The Magic World of the Xhosa,* pp. 97–98.

34. Elliott, *The Magic World of the Xhosa,* p. 100.

35. Hiltunen, *Witchcraft and Sorcery in Ovambo,* p. 57.

36. Gibson, Larson, and McGurk, *The Kavango Peoples,* p. 258.

37. Lye and Murray, *Transformations on the Highveld,* p. 127.

38. Elliott, *The Magic World of the Xhosa,* p. 115.

39. Elliott, *The Magic World of the Xhosa,* pp. 98–99.

40. Harriet Ngubane, *Body and Mind in Zulu Medicine.* London: Academic Press, 1971, pp. 58–59.

41. Ngubane, *Body and Mind in Zulu Medicine,* p. 59.

42. //Kabbo, quoted in Lewis-Williams, *Stories that Float from Afar,* p. 248.

43. Richard B. Lee, *The Dobe !Kung.* New York: Holt, Rinehart and Winston, 1984, pp. 106–107.

44. Barbara Tyrrell, *Tribal Peoples of Southern Africa,* p. 124.

45. Lye and Murray, *Transformations on the Highveld,* pp. 128–29.

46. Lye and Murray, *Tranformations on the Highveld,* pp. 128–29.

Chapter 6: Southern Africa Today—Problems and Promises

47. Colin Legum, *Africa Since Independence.* Bloomington: Indiana University Press, 1999, p. 55.
48. Morag Bell, *Contemporary Africa: Development, Culture and the State,* London: Longman Group, 1986, pp. 182–83.
49. Basil Davidson, *Modern Africa: a Social and Political History.* London: Longman Group, 1994, p. 221.
50. Davan Maharaj, "Angola and Rebels Sign Cease-Fire Agreement," *Los Angeles Times*, April 5, 2002, p. A3.
51. Maharaj, "Angola and Rebels Sign Cease-Fire Agreement," p. A3.
52. April A. Gordon and Donald L. Gordon, eds., *Understanding Contemporary Africa.* Boulder, CO: Lynne Rienner Publishers, 1996, p. 179.
53. Gordon and Gordon, *Understanding Contemporary Africa*, p. 181.
54. Research Staff of South African Institute of Race Relations, *South Africa Survey 1999/2000 Millennium Edition.* Johannesburg: South African Institute of Race Relations, 1999, p. 205.
55. Gordon and Gordon, *Understanding Contemporary Africa,* p. 189.

For Further Reading

Books

Ettagale Blauer and Jason Laure, *Enchantment of the World: Swaziland.* New York: Children's Press, 1996. This is an informational book about the history, cultures, geography, economy, and politics of one of southern Africa's smallest nations.

Patricia Cheney, *Land and People of Zimbabwe.* New York: J.B. Lippincott, 1990. This volume covers the history of Zimbabwe through easy-to-read chronologies, first-person accounts of historical events, and black-and-white photographs.

Amiran Gonen, ed., *Peoples of the World: Customs and Cultures.* Danbury, CT: Grolier Educational, 1998. This ten-volume encyclopedia of world peoples and their cultures includes such southern African cultures as the Xhosa and Zulu.

Jason Laure and Ettagale Blauer, *Enchantment of the World: Mozambique.* New York: Children's Press, 1995. This book offers a comprehensive view of the nation of Mozambique, including segments about the people and cultures, politics, history, and economy.

Ike Rosmarin, *Cultures of the World: South Africa.* New York: Marshall Cavendish, 1993. Simple text about the many cultures inhabiting the nation of South Africa is illustrated with color photographs on every page.

Sean Sheehan, *Cultures of the World: Zimbabwe.* New York: Marshall Cavendish, 1993. This full-color volume on the peoples, cultures, and lifestyles of Zimbabwe includes photographs, charts, and maps.

Websites

Africa: The Art of a Continent: Southern Africa (http://artnetweb. com). This site contains information on early rock art formations in southern Africa, as well as other art-related issues.

Africa Online: Kids Only (www.africaonline.com). This website for kids covers information on a variety of Africa-related topics.

Colonial Africa in the Electronic Passport (www.mrdowling.com). This website includes historical information about colonial and modern Africa.

!ke e/Xarra //ke (http://library.thinkquest.org). This site teaches some of the basics of Khoisan, or San language, pronunciation.

Southern Africa Wildlife Trust (www.africanwildlifetrust.org). This site features information about wildlife conservation issues and solutions in southern Africa.

United Nations International Children's Emergency Fund (www.unicef.org). This website features information on UNICEF efforts and children's needs and services throughout the world, including the legacy of apartheid, floods and other natural disasters, education, and diseases affecting children.

Zimmedia: Southern African Resources (zimmedia@africaonline.co.zw). This website, based in Zimbabwe, provides links with a variety of resources throughout the region, including the arts, government, and environmental agencies.

Works Consulted

Books

Morag Bell, *Contemporary Africa: Development, Culture and the State*. London: Longman Group, 1986. This political analysis examines the economic development and political culture of modern-day Africa.

Surendra Bhana and Bridglal Pachai, eds., *A Documentary History of Indian South Africans*. Cape Town, South Africa: David Philip, 1984. This history of the Indians of South Africa uses first person accounts and historical documents to illustrate South Asian life in the region.

Fred Bridgland, *Jonas Savimbi: A Key to Africa*. Edinburgh, Scotland: Mainstream Publishing Co., 1986. Bridgland, a journalist, documents the life and times of Jonas Savimbi, rebel leader of Angola, from his education as a child through his development as an important political figure in the region.

Basil Davidson, *Modern Africa: a Social and Political History*. London: Longman Group, 1994. Part history, part political analysis, this book looks at modern Africa from a historical viewpoint and helps the reader learn how Africa came to be in its modern state.

Aubrey Elliott, *The Magic World of the Xhosa*. London: William Collins Sons & Co., 1975. This photo-documentary examines the cultural and religious practices of the Xhosa ethnic group.

Gordon D. Gibson, Thomas J. Larson, and Cecilia R. McGurk, *The Kavango Peoples*. Wiesbaden, Germany: Franz Steiner, 1981. Three different anthropologists study the disparate groups of the Okavango region of Botswana, Angola, and Namibia, looking at the lifestyle and cultures of the people who live there.

April A. Gordon and Donald L. Gordon, eds., *Understanding Contemporary Africa*. Boulder, CO: Lynne Rienner Publishers, 1996.

This book examines many different issues in contemporary Africa—health care, politics, and the economy—to help the reader understand the problems and promises of the region.

Martin Hall, *The Changing Past: Farmers, Kings and Traders in Southern Africa, 200–1860*. Cape Town, South Africa: David Philip, 1987. Historian Hall pieces together the various kingdoms of southern Africa from anthropological and archeological data.

Maija Hiltunen, *Witchcraft and Sorcery in Ovambo*. Helsinki: The Finnish Anthropological Society, 1986. An anthropological study of some of the religious practices of the Ovambo of Namibia, this book offers eyewitness observations of important cultural rituals.

IDAF Research, Information and Publications Department, Namibia, "The Facts." London: International Defense and Aid Fund for Southern Africa Publications, 1989. This pamphlet, written prior to the independence of Namibia, offers a rebel's-eye view of life in Namibia.

Richard B. Lee, *The Dobe !Kung*. New York: Holt, Rinehart and Winston, 1984. This classic study of the Dobe !Kung Bushmen of the Kalihari is an engaging eyewitness account of a dying lifestyle.

Colin Legum, *Africa Since Independence*. Bloomington: Indiana University Press, 1999. A political analysis of the independent states of southern Africa, this book looks at the interrelations between the economies, cultures, and policies of the region's nations.

J.D. Lewis-Williams, ed., *Stories that Float from Afar: Ancestral Folklore of the San of South Africa*. College Station: Texas A&M University Press, 2000. These stories, handed down for centuries by San Bushmen of South Africa, reveal the San's beliefs in their own words.

William F. Lye and Colin Murray, *Transformations on the High-veld: The Tswana and Southern Sotho*. Totowa, NJ: Barnes and Noble, 1980. This anthropological study examines life in the past and present among the Tswana and Sotho on the grasslands of southern Africa.

Philip Mayer, *Townsmen or Tribesmen: Conservatism and the Process of Urbanization in a South African City.* Cape Town, South Africa: Oxford University Press, 1962. Mayer, a sociologist, looks at the experience of Xhosa tribesmen living in an urban area.

Henning Melber, comp., *Our Namibia: A Social Studies Textbook.* London: Zed Books, 1986. This textbook, written for Namibian children living abroad before independence, gives a uniquely Namibian perspective to the history, cultures, and conditions of the region.

H.O. Monning, *The Pedi.* Pretoria, South Africa: J.L. Van Schaik, 1967. Anthropologist Monning examines the historical and cultural background of the Pedi of South Africa.

Jocelyn Murray, ed., *Cultural Atlas of Africa.* Oxford, England: Phaidon Press, 1981. Through detailed maps, photographs, and descriptions, this book documents the human geography of the entire continent of Africa.

Harriet Ngubane, *Body and Mind in Zulu Medicine.* London: Academic Press, 1971. Zulu anthropologist Harriet Ngubane examines Zulu views of health and medicine in this academic study.

J.D. Omer-Cooper, *History of Southern Africa.* London: James Currey, 1987. This comprehensive history covers prehistoric southern Africa through the apartheid era and beyond. Photos, period etchings, and cartoons illustrate insightful analysis.

Research Staff of South African Institute of Race Relations, *South Africa Survey 1999/2000 Millennium Edition.* Johannesburg: South African Institute of Race Relations, 1999. A yearly report, the *South Africa Survey* uses surveys and statistics to provide accurate data on every imaginable aspect of South African life.

Kevin Shillington, *History of Africa.* New York: St. Martin's Press, 1995. A complete history of Africa, with photos, maps, and charts, this book jumps around the continent to provide a thematic and geographic approach to history.

———, *A History of Southern Africa.* Essex, England: Longman Group, 1987. This regional history offers details and anecdotes about the people, ethnic groups, battles, and alliances that are important to the people of the region.

Jiro Tanaka, *The San: Hunter-Gatherers of the Kalahari.* Tokyo: University of Tokyo Press, 1980. This academic study of the San Bushmen examines their lifestyle and culture in modern times.

Elizabeth Marshall Thomas, *The Harmless People.* New York: Vintage Books, 1989. This classic narrative about the lives of the San Bushmen is a friendly look at the people who live the lifestyle called hunting-gathering.

Barbara Tyrrell, *Tribal Peoples of Southern Africa.* Cape Town, South Africa: Books of Africa, 1968. Barbara Tyrrell wrote and illustrated this coffee-table book during travels around the southern African region in the 1950s and 1960s. Full-color illustrations.

UNESCO *General History of Africa.* 8 Vols. London: Heinemann and the University of California Press, 1981–1993. A major publishing project of the United Nations Educational, Scientific, and Cultural Organization, this highly regarded work offers an extremely detailed view of African history and culture from prehistory through the present.

Al J. Venter, *Coloured: A Profile of Two Million South Africans.* Cape Town, South Africa: Human and Rousseau, 1974. This engaging account examines the lives of mixed-race South Africans from many different viewpoints: economic, historical, political, and personal.

Marq de Villiers, *White Tribe Dreaming.* New York: Viking Penguin, 1987. Marq de Villiers tells his family's history as early South African settlers within the larger context of Afrikaner history and the development of Afrikaner culture.

Frank Robert Vivelo, *The Herero of Western Botswana.* St. Paul, MN: West Publishing Co., 1977. Vivelo, a historian, examines the history and cultures of the formerly pastoral Herero people.

Periodicals

Davan Maharaj, "Angola and Rebels Sign Cease-Fire Agreement," *Los Angeles Times*, April 5, 2002. This article is about the Angolan cease-fire which was made possible by the death of rebel leader Jonas Savimbi.

Ann M. Simmons, "Lesotho: Educating Young Herders." *Los Angeles Times*, June 9, 2002. This article paints a portrait of the lives of young herd boys in Lesotho, and their government's belief that school is a better occupation for boys than herding.

————, "South African Whites Say Deck is Stacked Against Them." *Los Angeles Times*, June 19, 2002. In this article, Afrikaners have their say about the effects of affirmative action on their lives and livelihoods in South Africa.

Internet Sources

Amnesty International, "Female Genital Mutilation," 1997. www.amnesty.org.

World Health Organization (WHO), "Pollution-Related Diseases Kill Millions of Children A Year," 2002. www.who.int.

Zimbabwe Independent, "Renewed fear grips farming sector," March 22, 2002. www.theindependent.co.zw.

Index

Picture Credits

About the Author

Cynthia L. Jenson-Elliott first became interested in Africa while studying African history as a college student at Bowdoin College in Maine. In 1984 she spent five months in Kenya and Tanzania through the St. Lawrence University Semester in Kenya. During that time she lived with many different ethnic groups throughout Kenya. Ms. Jenson-Elliott holds a master's degree in education and has worked as a teacher, environmental and museum educator, and educational writer. She is currently a stay-at-home mom. This is her second book for middle school students.